# BRIDGES®
## IN MATHEMATICS

SECOND EDITION
# HOME CONNECTIONS

GRADE
**K**

Published by  The **MATH LEARNING CENTER** *Salem, Oregon*

**Bridges in Mathematics Second Edition Kindergarten Home Connections**

The Bridges in Mathematics Kindergarten package consists of:

Bridges in Mathematics Kindergarten Teachers Guide Units 1–8

Bridges in Mathematics Kindergarten Assessment Guide

*Bridges in Mathematics Kindergarten Teacher Masters*

Bridges in Mathematics Kindergarten Student Book

Bridges in Mathematics Kindergarten Home Connections

*Bridges in Mathematics Kindergarten Teacher Masters Answer Key*

*Bridges in Mathematics Kindergarten Student Book Answer Key*

*Bridges in Mathematics Kindergarten Home Connections Answer Key*

Bridges in Mathematics Kindergarten Components & Manipulatives

*Bridges Educator Site*

Work Place Games & Activities

Number Corner Kindergarten Teachers Guide Volumes 1–3

*Number Corner Kindergarten Teacher Masters*

Number Corner Kindergarten Student Book

*Number Corner Kindergarten Teacher Masters Answer Key*

*Number Corner Kindergarten Student Book Answer Key*

Number Corner Kindergarten Components & Manipulatives

Word Resource Cards

*Digital resources noted in italics.*

The Math Learning Center, PO Box 12929, Salem, Oregon 97309. Tel 1 (800) 575-8130
www.mathlearningcenter.org

Prepared for publication using Mac OS X and Adobe Creative Suite.
Printed in the United States of America.

To reorder Home Connections, refer to number 2B0HC5 (package of 5 sets).

Bridges Kindergarten Home Connections Online PDF (2B0HC)
19100_LSCCOM
Updated 2019-01-01.

*Bridges in Mathematics* is a standards-based K–5 curriculum that provides a unique blend of concept development and skills practice in the context of problem solving. It incorporates Number Corner, a collection of daily skill-building activities for students.

The Math Learning Center is a nonprofit organization serving the education community. Our mission is to inspire and enable individuals to discover and develop their mathematical confidence and ability. We offer innovative and standards-based professional development, curriculum, materials, and resources to support learning and teaching. To find out more, visit us at www.mathlearningcenter.org.

ISBN 978-1-60262-304-0

Bridges Kindergarten
# Home Connections

# Unit 7
## Weight & Place Value

# Unit 8
## Computing & Measuring with Frogs & Bugs

NAME Aliza Berger                    DATE

 **Butterflies & Dots** page 1 of 2

## Butterflies 0–4

Count the butterflies in each frame. Trace the numbers.

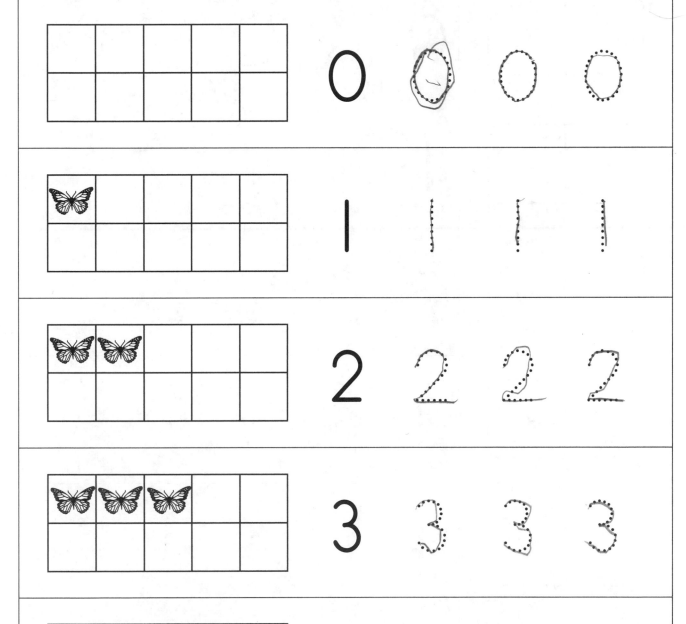

*(continued on next page)*

    © The Math Learning Center | mathlearningcenter.org

**NAME** | **DATE**

## Butterflies & Dots page 2 of 2

## How Many Dots?

Count the dots on each domino. Trace the numbers.

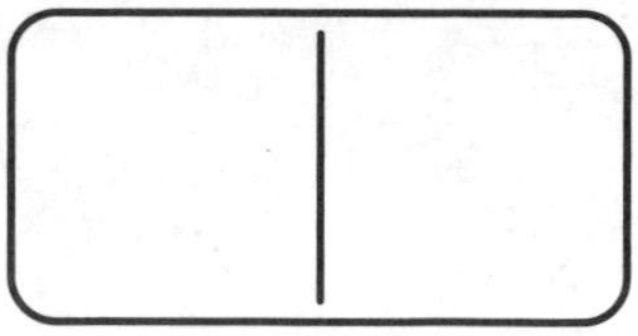

| | |
|---|---|
| [domino: blank \| blank] | 0  0  0  0  0 |
| 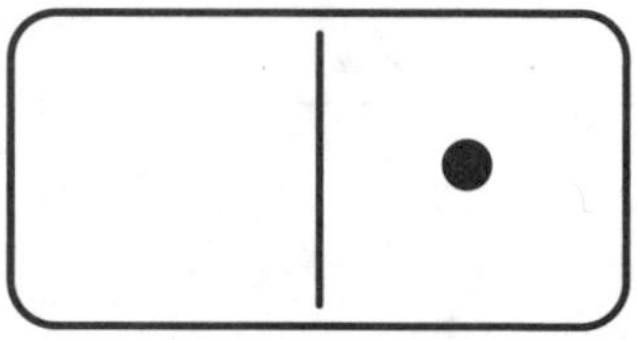 [domino: blank \| 1 dot] | 1  1  1  1  1 |
| [domino: 1 dot \| 1 dot] | 2  2  2  2  2 |
| [domino: 1 dot \| 2 dots] | 3  3  3  3  3 |
| [domino: 2 dots \| 2 dots] | 4  4  4  4  4 |
| [domino: 1 dot \| 3 dots] | 5  5  5  5  5 |

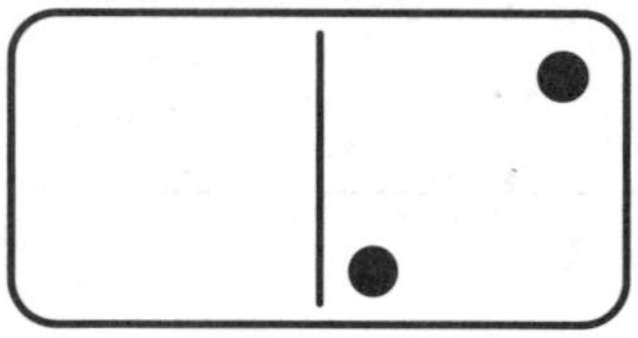

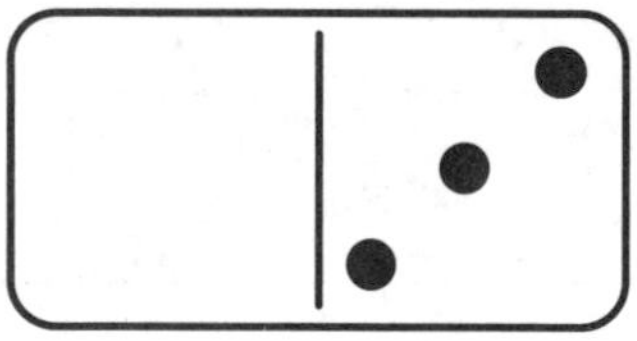

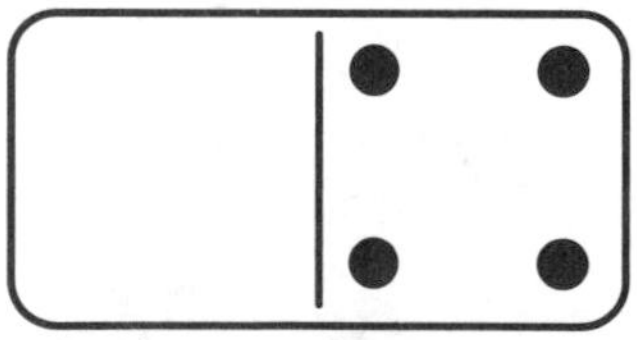

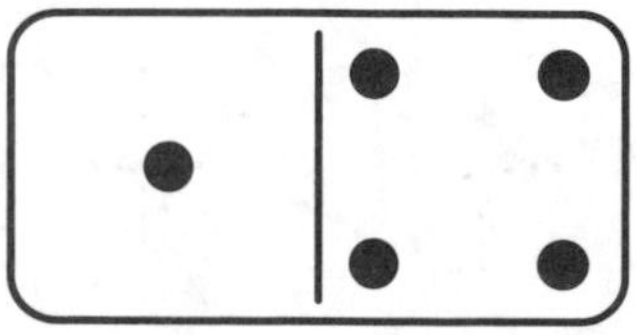

5  5

2

NAME                                                    | DATE

 **Count & Match** page 1 of 2

## Find the Match

Draw a line to match the ten-frame to the domino with the same number of dots.
Trace the numbers.

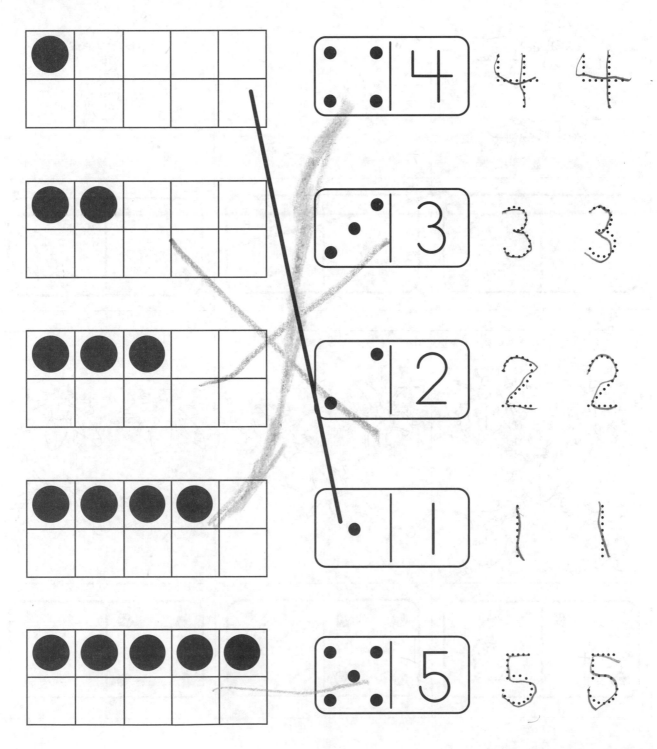

*(continued on next page)*

    3

NAME | DATE

## Count & Match page 2 of 2

## Bugs in Boxes

Count the bugs in each box. Draw a line to the domino that has the same number. Trace the numbers.

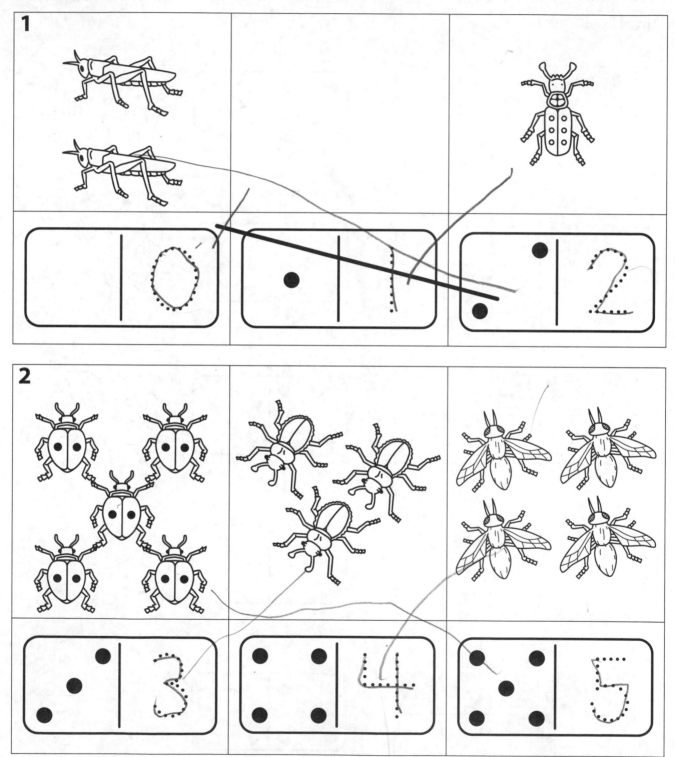

4

**NAME** | **DATE**

 **More Count & Match** page 1 of 2

## Sets & Numbers Match

**1** Draw a line to match each set to the number that tells how many. Trace the number three times.

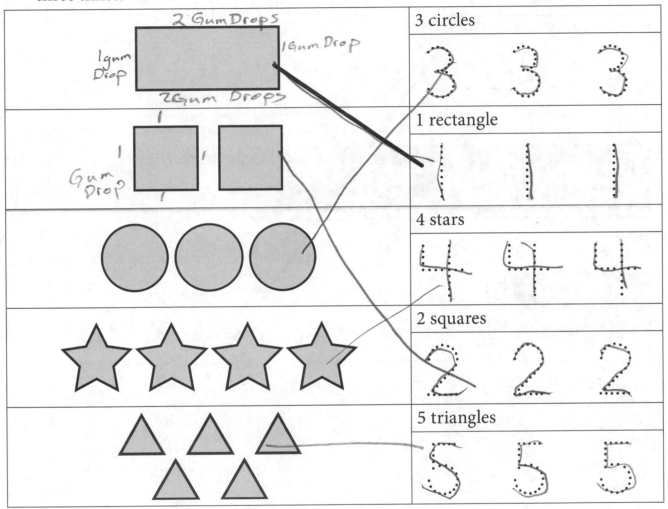

**2** Trace the numbers below.

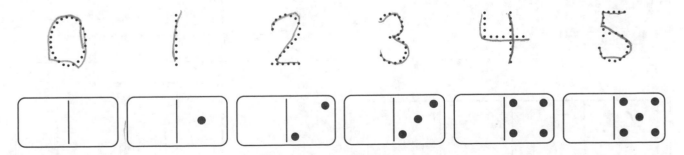

*(continued on next page)*

NAME | DATE

## More Count & Match page 2 of 2

## Counting Cubes

Color the cubes as indicated. Draw a line to the domino that has the same number. Trace the numbers.

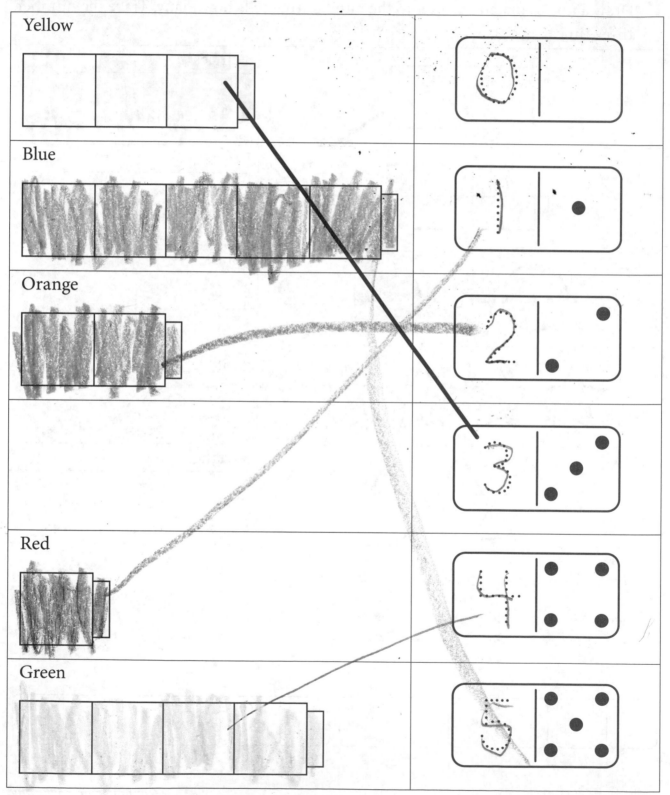

**Shapes & Numbers**

**1**  Color the number of shapes as indicated below:

Color 5 squares:

Color 4 rectangles:

Color 2 triangles:

Color 3 circles:

**2**  Trace the numbers.

**Bug Patterns** page 1 of 2

## Note to Families

This Home Connection shows four different bug patterns. Your child will figure out how the pattern is repeating and how to complete it.

## Materials

- Bug Patterns, pages 1 & 2
- scissors
- glue or tape

## Instructions

**1** Cut out the bug boxes at the bottom of page 2 of this assignment, and sort them into two piles—ladybugs and spiders.

**2** Look at the pattern at the top of the worksheet. How does it repeat?

**3** Place bugs into the empty boxes to complete the pattern.

**4** When you are sure the pattern is correct, glue or tape the bugs into the boxes.

**5** Do the same for the other three patterns.

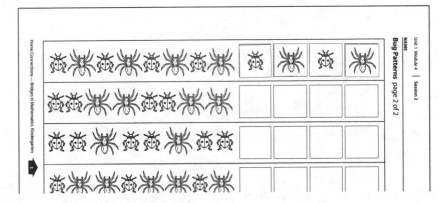

**6** Return your paper to your teacher when you are done.

## Salt Box Numerals page 1 of 2

**Note to Families**

This Home Connection is a fun way to practice writing numerals.

## Materials

- Salt Box Numerals, pages 1 & 2
- a shallow cake pan or cookie sheet
- salt (enough to cover the bottom of the pan in a thin layer)
- scissors
- envelope to store cards

## Instructions

**1** Cut apart the cards from page 2 of this assignment.

**2** Have an adult help you pour a thin layer of salt in the pan.

**3** Choose a numeral card. The arrow shows you where to start.

**4** Use your pointer finger to write the numeral again and again the salt until the pan is filled.

**5** Show someone in your family.

**6** Gently shake the pan to "erase" the numerals.

**7** Choose another card and start again.

**8** Use at least 4 or 5 of the cards each time you practice. Store them in the envelope.

14

NAME | DATE

## Salt Box Numerals page 2 of 2

**Bugs Bingo** page 1 of 3

## Note to Families

When you play this game with your child, be sure to watch (and ask about) how they count the bugs. Encourage them to try different ways—counting by 1s or by 2s, seeing the line of 5 and counting on (5…6, 7, 8), seeing 5 in one row and 3 in the next and adding them, and so on.

## Materials

- Bugs Bingo, pages 1–3
- scissors
- game markers (such as pennies, cereal pieces, dry beans, small pieces of paper)
- envelope (to store game cards)

## Instructions

**1** Cut around the nine ten-frame bug cards on page 2 and store them in an envelope.

**2** Cut apart the bingo boards on page 3 so you have two.

**3** Each player gets one bingo board and a handful of game markers.

**4** Take turns picking a bug card.

- How many bugs are on the card?
- How did you count them?
- Is there another way to count them?
- **CHALLENGE** How many more to make 10?

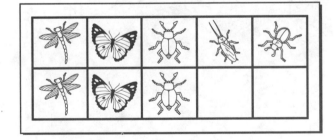

**5** Cover that number on your bingo board.

**6** The first player to get three markers in a row in any direction wins the game.

**7** Play the game several times this week.

*(continued on next page)*

## Bugs Bingo page 2 of 3

*(continued on next page)*

**Bugs Bingo** page 3 of 3

| | | |
|---|---|---|
| 6 | 10 | 7 |
| 4 | 9 | 8 |
| 2 | 3 | 5 |

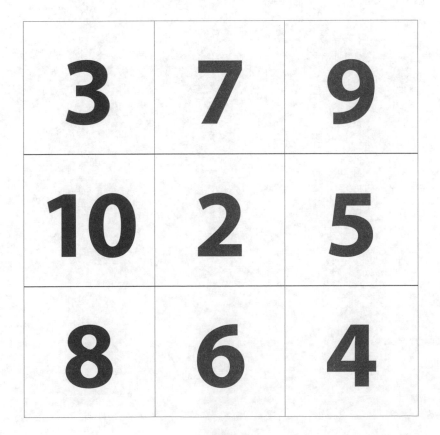

| | | |
|---|---|---|
| 3 | 7 | 9 |
| 10 | 2 | 5 |
| 8 | 6 | 4 |

NAME | DATE

 **Count & Compare Butterflies** page 1 of 4

**Note to Families**

This card game is like the old game "War." Players should figure out more than one way to count the butterflies on each card.

## Materials

- Count & Compare Butterflies, pages 1–4
- scissors
- envelope (to store game cards)
- paperclip and a pencil (to use as a spinner)

## Instructions

Use your pencil and paperclip to make an arrow for the spinner. Place the pencil, point down, through one end of the paperclip and onto the dot at the middle of the spinner.

**1** Cut apart the butterfly cards on pages 2 and 3, and store them in an envelope.

**2** Take turns pulling out a butterfly card.

**3** Count the butterflies.
*How did you count them?*
*Can you count them another way?*

It's 5! 2 + 3 makes 5.
It's like 2 + 2 and 1 more.

I've got 6. I can tell 'cause
it's 1 more than 5.
It could be 2 and 4, too.

**4** Who has more butterflies on their card? Less?

**5** Put the cards in the "more" and "less" boxes on the game board (page 4).

**6** Spin the paperclip-and-pencil spinner to see which card wins. The winner takes both cards.

**7** Repeat steps 2–6 until you use all the cards.

**8** Players count their cards. The player with more cards places them in the "more" box, and the player with fewer cards places them in the "less" box.

**9** Spin one last time to see who wins the game.

*(continued on next page)*

## Count & Compare Butterflies page 2 of 4

© The Math Learning Center | mathlearningcenter.org

(continued on next page)

## Count & Compare Butterflies page 3 of 4

(continued on next page)

## Count & Compare Butterflies page 4 of 4

less

Just the same!

Put them back in the pile.

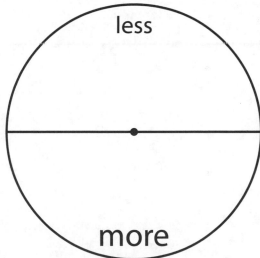

less

more

more

NAME |DATE

 **Ladybugs & Dots** page 1 of 2

## Ladybugs 5–9

Count the ladybugs in each ten-frame. Trace the numerals.

5　5　5　5

6　6　6　6

7　7　7　7

8　8　8　8

9　9　9　9

*(continued on next page)*

**Ladybugs & Dots** page 2 of 2

## Find the Match

Draw a line to match the ten-frame to the domino with the same number of dots.
Trace the numerals.

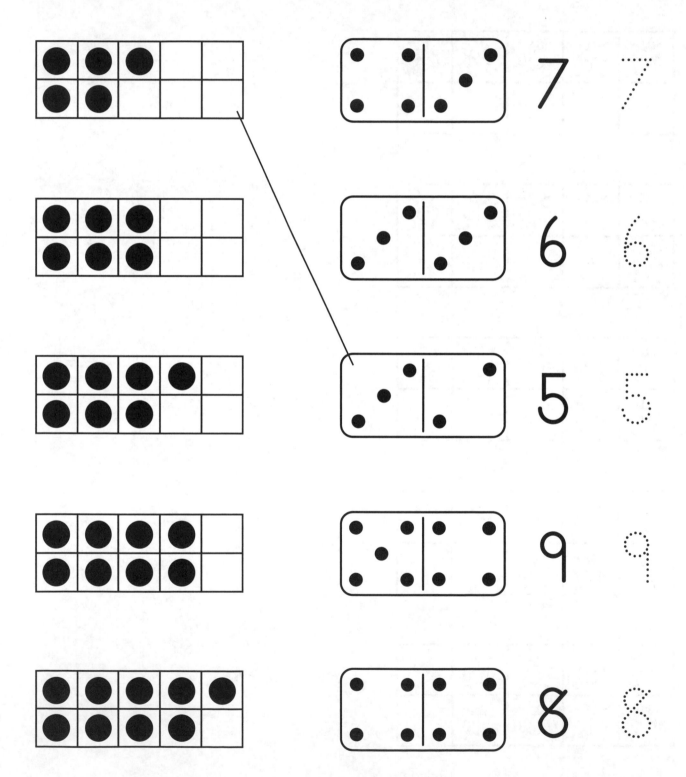

**Count & Match to Ten** page 1 of 2

## More Dots

Count the dots on each domino. Trace the numerals.

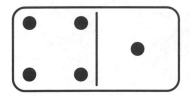 5    5    5    5    5

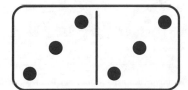 6    6    6    6    6

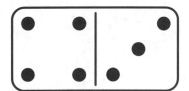 7    7    7    7    7

 8    8    8    8    8

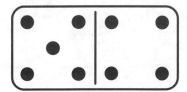 9    9    9    9

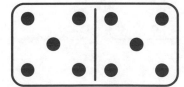 10    10    10    10    10

*(continued on next page)*

NAME _____ | DATE _____

## Count & Match to Ten page 2 of 2

## More Bugs in Boxes

Count the bugs in each box. Draw a line to the domino that has the same number. Trace the numerals.

**1**

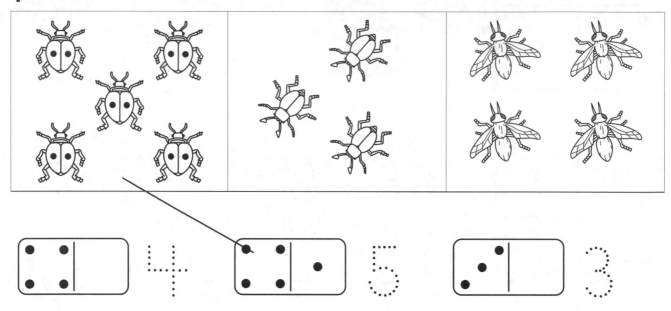

**2**

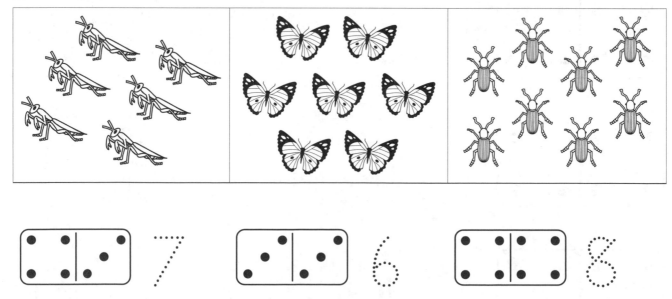

NAME | DATE

 **Toothpick Pictures & Tallying** page 1 of 2

**Note to Families**

Encourage your child to play with the toothpicks, make pictures or alphabet letters, and perhaps even glue a creation down. Then they can get to work on the Toothpick Tallying.

## Materials

- Toothpick Pictures & Tallying, pages 1 & 2
- small handful of toothpicks
- scissors
- glue or tape (optional)

## Instructions

**1** Take a few minutes to just play with the toothpicks and make some pictures or alphabet letters.

**2** Cut apart the six cards on page 2. Can you read the numbers?

**3** Lay out the cards in order from 4 to 9.

   **a** Carefully set 4 toothpicks out on the first card.

   **b** Count out 5 toothpicks for the second card. Lay out the first 4 and lay the 5th one diagonally over the others.

Is it easy to see the "gate" of five?

**4** Keep going until you have set out toothpicks on all the cards. Make a gate of 5 each time.

**5** Do you see how you can either count them one by one or think about them as 5 and some more?

**6** Save the cards for another day and try again. Can you predict how each group will look before you build it with toothpicks?

**7** **CHALLENGE** If this seems easy for your child, challenge her to build some bigger numbers. For example, she could build 12 with 2 groups of 5 and 2 more.

*(continued on next page)*

NAME | DATE

**Toothpick Pictures & Tallying** page 2 of 2

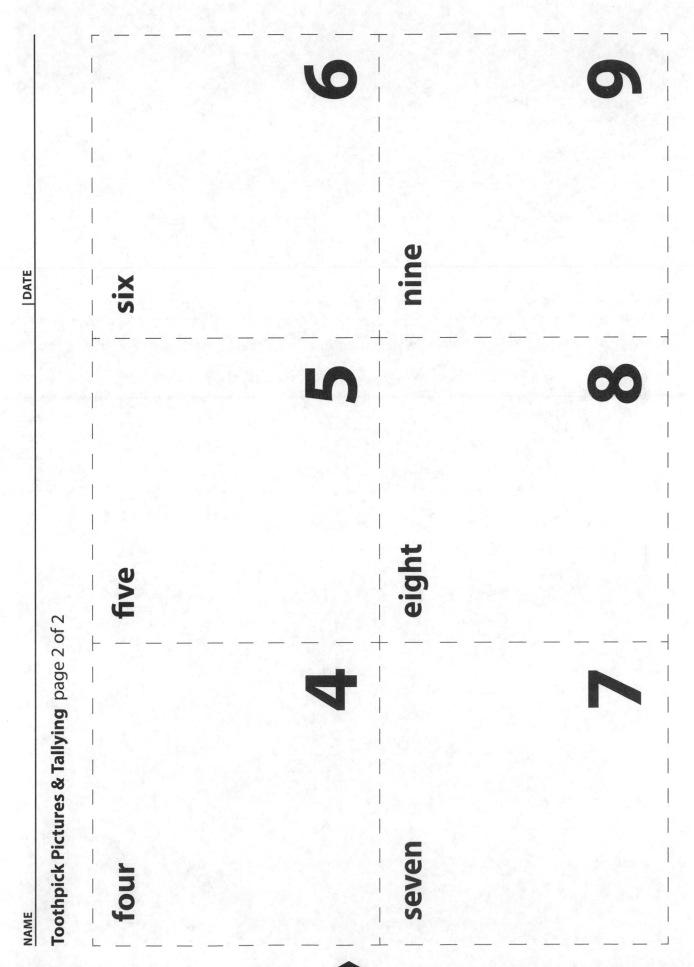

four

five

4

5

six

6

seven

eight

nine

7

8

9

**Which Bug Will Win?** page 1 of 2

### Note to Families

We've been playing this game in school. Students use a different spinner each time they play and then think about the results for each bug. Does one bug win because of the spinner used?

## Materials

- Which Bug Will Win? pages 1 & 2
- paperclip and pencil (to use as a spinner)

## Instructions

Use your pencil and paperclip to make an arrow for the spinner. Place the pencil, point down, through one end of the paperclip and onto the dot at the middle of the spinner.

**1** Look at Spinner 1. Which bug do you think will win?

**2** Spin the spinner over and over. In the first graph, record the results for each spin with an X until one column is filled to the top.

- Which bug won?
- Why do you think that happened?
- Will you get the same results another time?

**3** Play again using Spinner 1. Spin and record the results on the second graph.

**4** Play two times using Spinner 2. Record the results on the graphs below.

- Which bug do you think will win?
- Which bug won?
- Why do you think that happened?
- Do you think your classmates got the same results?

**5** Return your paper to your teacher.

*(continued on next page)*

NAME _____ | DATE _____

## Which Bug Will Win? page 2 of 2

**1**

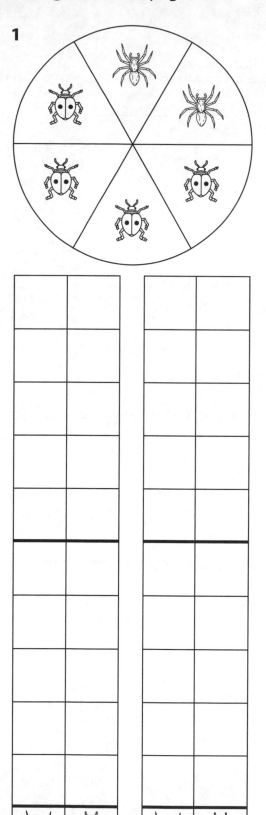

**2**

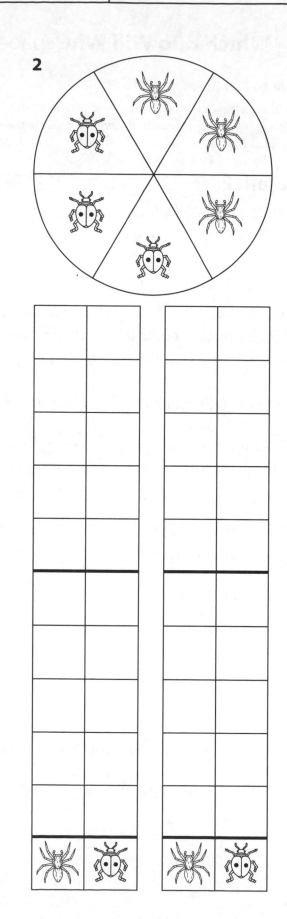

**Draw & Dot-to-Dot** page 1 of 2

**1** Trace the numerals.

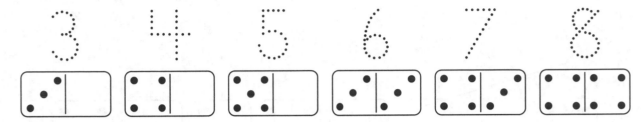

**2** Draw the items below.

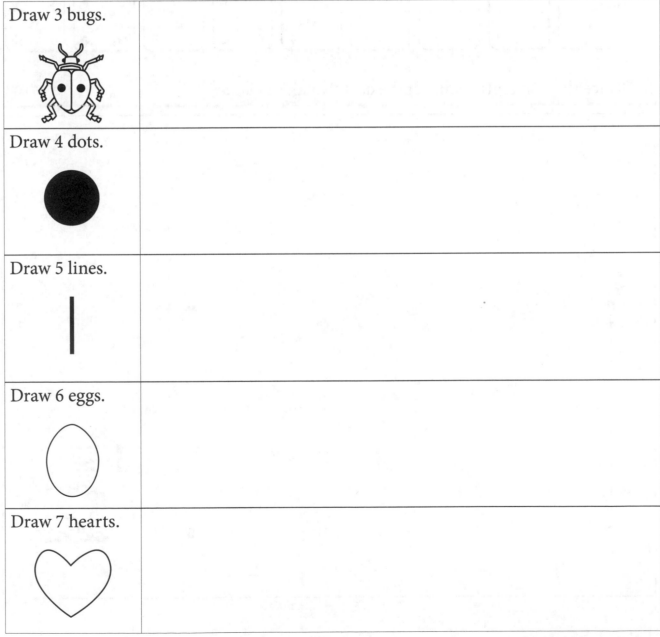

*(continued on next page)*

**Draw & Dot-to-Dot** page 2 of 2

**3**  Trace the numerals. Draw a line from each numeral to the matching domino.

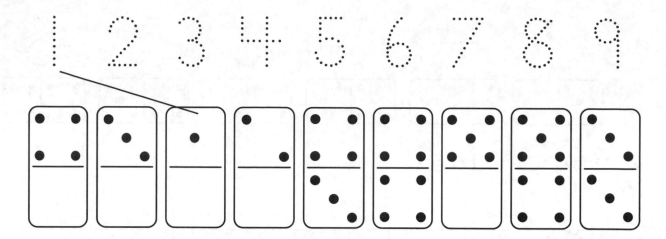

**4**  Trace the numerals. Connect the dots to make a picture.

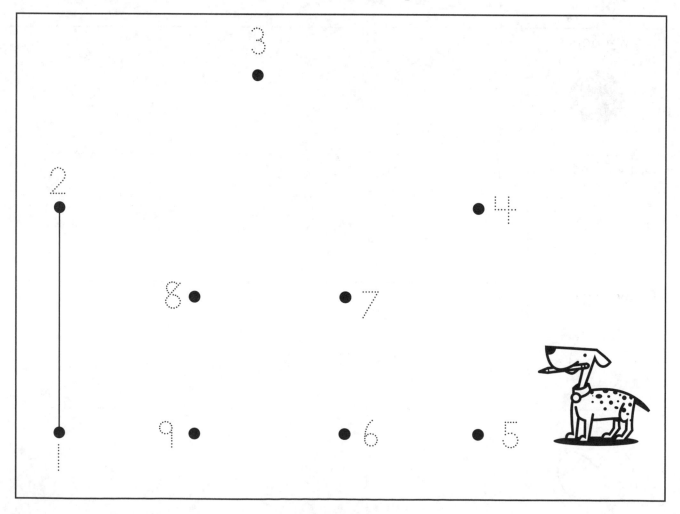

NAME | DATE

 **Pattern Block Butterflies** page 1 of 3

### Note for Families

This activity challenges students to find different ways to fit paper pattern block shapes into a butterfly design. Please help your child cut out the paper pattern block shapes.

## Materials

- Pattern Block Butterflies, pages 1–3
- pattern block paper shapes (yellow hexagons, red trapezoids, green triangles, blue rhombuses, orange squares, and white rhombuses; sent home from school)
- scissors
- glue
- envelope (to store extra cutout pattern blocks)

## Instructions

**1** Work together to cut out some paper pattern blocks. (Save extras for future Home Connections.)

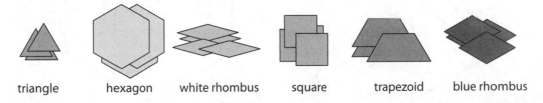

triangle      hexagon      white rhombus      square      trapezoid      blue rhombus

**2** Use the paper pattern block shapes to fill the butterfly on page 2. Use any shapes you wish that fit.

- Try not to leave any holes or gaps.
- Make the shapes fit within the lines.
- You may need to turn or flip the paper shapes.

**3** You can glue the shapes to the paper after you find a solution, or glue them as you go.

**4** Count how many of each pattern block shape you used. Write the number in the chart at the bottom of the butterfly worksheet.

**5** Find a different way to fill the butterfly on page 3. Glue the paper pattern blocks down. Fill in the chart at the bottom of the page.

*(continued on next page)*

## Pattern Block Butterflies page 2 of 3

| Pattern Block Shape | Yellow Hexagon | Red Trapezoid | Green Triangle | Orange Square | Blue Rhombus | White Rhombus |
|---|---|---|---|---|---|---|
| How many did you use? | | | | | | |

How many did you use in all? _____

*(continued on next page)*

NAME _____ | DATE _____

## Pattern Block **Butterflies** page 3 of 3

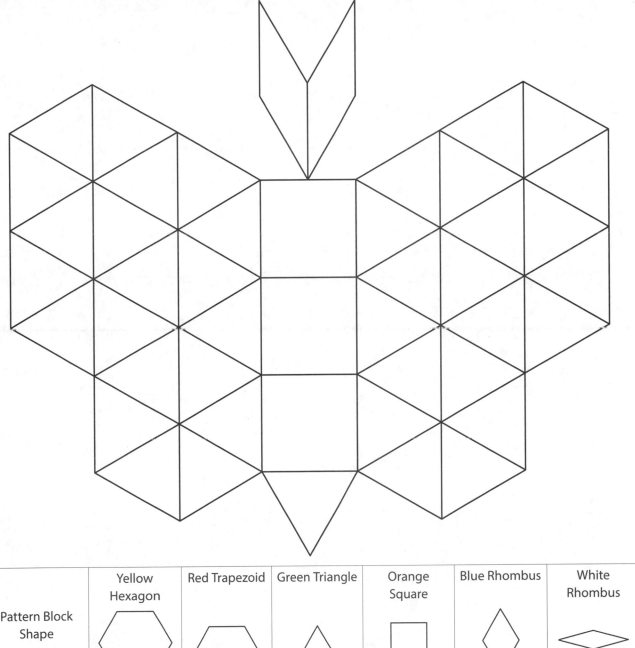

| Pattern Block Shape | Yellow Hexagon | Red Trapezoid | Green Triangle | Orange Square | Blue Rhombus | White Rhombus |
|---|---|---|---|---|---|---|
| How many did you use? | | | | | | |

How many did you use in all? _____

NAME | DATE

 **Tally & Number Match Game** page 1 of 6

## Note to Families
Play a matching game with the tally cards and the number cards. If your child needs practice recognizing the groups of tally sticks without counting, try "flashing" the cards—showing them for just three seconds. The two worksheets offer more practice in counting and writing numbers.

## Materials
- Tally & Number Match Game, pages 1–6
- scissors
- envelope (to store game cards)

**1** Cut apart the tally and number cards on pages 3 and 4.

**2** Lay all of the number cards face-up on one side and all of the tally cards face-up on the other side.

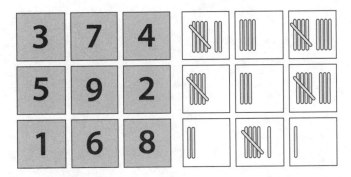

**3** Can you find the matching pairs?

**4** Once finding the matching pairs feels easy, turn all of the cards face-down.

**5** Take turns turning one card from each group face-up. Is it a matching pair?
- If it is, take those cards and take another turn.
- If they don't match, turn them back over and give your partner a turn.
- Try to remember where each card is located.

**6** The player with the most cards at the end of the game wins.

*(continued on next page)*

**47**

## Tally & Number Match Game page 2 of 6

**7** CHALLENGE

- If your child can easily match the tally cards with the number cards, go to the "face-down" version of the game right away.

- Another challenging activity would be to put the tally cards in order from greatest to least and the number cards from least to greatest.

**8** Play the game a few times this week. Save the cards so you can play again in a few weeks.

**9** Have your child complete the worksheets on pages 5 and 6, and return them to the teacher.

*(continued on next page)*

NAME | DATE

## Tally & Number Match Game  page 3 of 6

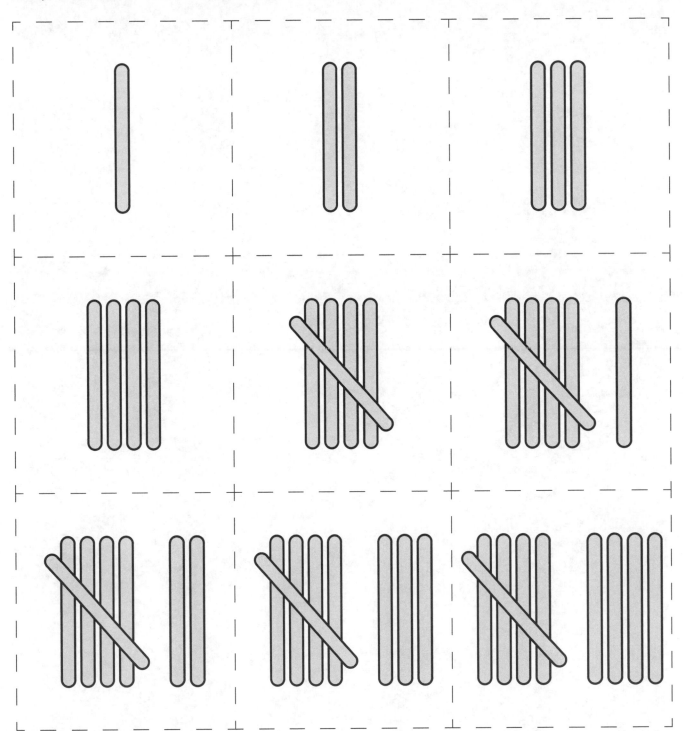

(continued on next page)

NAME                                                              | DATE

## Tally & Number Match Game  page 4 of 6

1  2  3

4  5  6

7  8  9

*(continued on next page)*

**NAME** | **DATE**

## Tally & Number Match Game page 5 of 6

Use the numbers and dominoes to help solve the problems below.

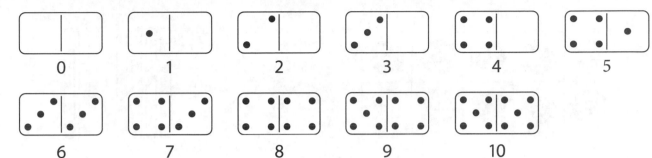

1    Count the number of sticks and record the number.

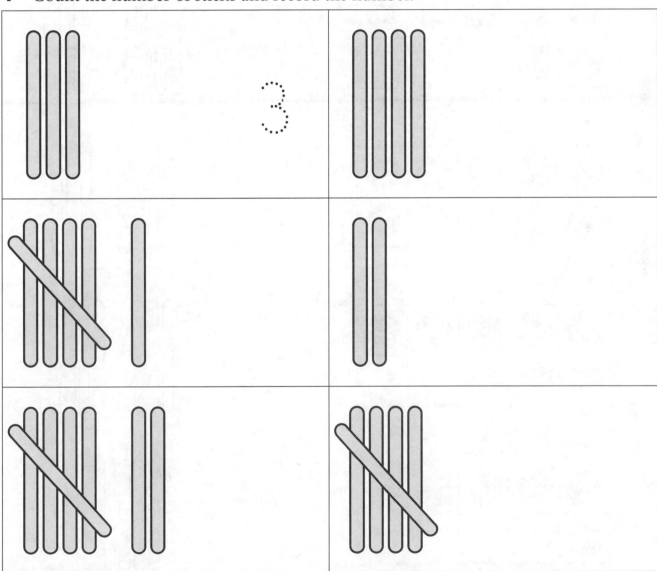

*(continued on next page)*

**NAME** | **DATE**

## Tally & Number Match Game page 6 of 6

Draw a line from the ten-frame to the tally sticks that match.

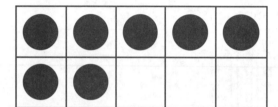 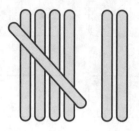

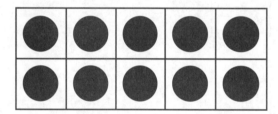 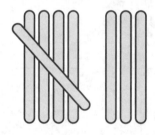

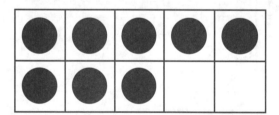 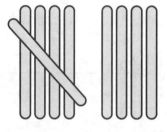

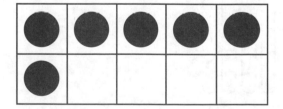 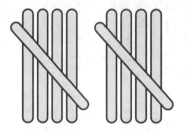

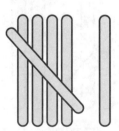

NAME _____ | DATE _____

 **Searching for Pairs** page 1 of 2

**Note to Families**

Have fun finding things around your house that come in pairs of 2. Write them down for your child. This will help your child learn to count by 2s and to learn about doubles. The worksheet on the back will provide more practice with 2s.

**1** Search your home for things that come in pairs—shoes, mittens, what else can you find? List them below.

_____    _____

_____    _____

_____    _____

**2** Now draw a picture of your favorite thing that you found that comes in pairs (a clock with two hands, your ballet slippers, Grandma's teacups).

**Searching for Pairs** page 2 of 2

## These Bikes Have Two Wheels

**3** Look at the bikes. How many bikes are in each picture? How many wheels are in each picture?

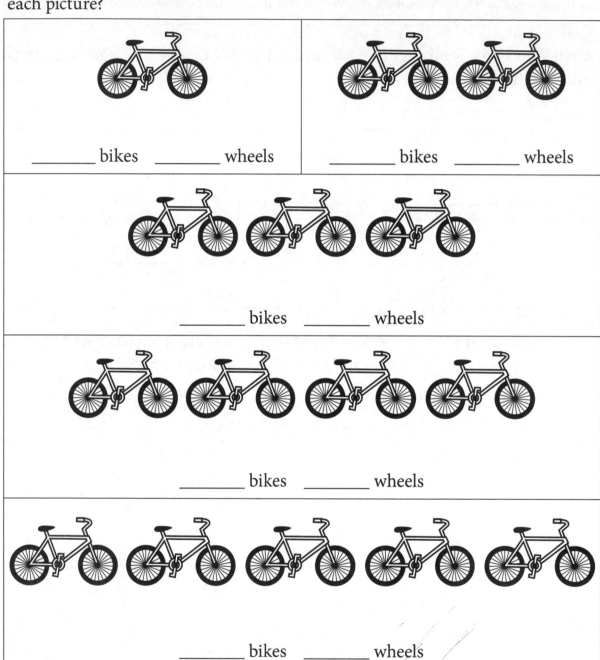

_____ bikes _____ wheels     _____ bikes _____ wheels

_____ bikes _____ wheels

_____ bikes _____ wheels

_____ bikes _____ wheels

**4** CHALLENGE Can you count the wheels by 2s?

| 2 | 4 | | | 10 | | | 16 | | |
|---|---|---|---|----|---|---|----|---|---|

**NAME** _____ | **DATE** _____

 # Butterfly Countdown page 1 of 5

## Note to Families

As you and your child act out counting down from 10 with paper butterflies, your child will be working with the big idea of subtracting 1. There are also two worksheets, one on addition and one on subtraction.

## Materials

- Butterfly Countdown, pages 1–5
- crayons (optional)
- scissors

## Instructions

**1** Color the page of butterfly cards if you like, and cut them out.

**2** Spread the 10 butterfly cards out in a line.

**3** Read the Butterfly Countdown poem one verse at a time, stopping before you say the final word (the number of butterflies left).

**4** Have your child take one butterfly away and ask, "How many are left?" Read the verse again, this time including the final word.

**5** Continue reading the poem until there are no more butterflies left.

**Note** Another way to do this, without reading the poem, would be to just start with 10 butterflies and take away 1 at a time, saying how many are left each time.

**6** Try some "mental math" now or at another time. (For example: Imagine 7 butterflies hovering over some flowers. If 1 flies away, how many will be left?)

**Note** If your child is more comfortable using the paper butterflies, be sure to get them out again.

**7** Have your child complete the worksheets on pages 4 and 5 and return them to the teacher.

*(continued on next page)*

**Butterfly Countdown** page 2 of 5

## Butterfly Countdown

Ten lovely butterflies over a garden fine,
One stopped to sip some nectar, then there were nine.

Nine lovely butterflies hovering over a gate,
One stopped to rest awhile, then there were eight.

Eight lovely butterflies flying toward heaven,
One found a tree in bloom, then there were seven.

Seven lovely butterflies, such a pretty mix,
One saw some flowers to sip, then there were six.

Six lovely butterflies saw a large beehive,
One stopped to find some honey, then there were five.

Five lovely butterflies flying near a door,
One saw some flowers for sale, then there were four.

Four lovely butterflies flying oh so free!
One stopped to see the pumpkins, then there were three.

Three lovely butterflies in the morning dew,
One stopped to see some plants, then there were two.

Two lovely butterflies in the midday sun,
One got a bit too hot, then there was one.

One lovely butterfly said, "Being lonely is no fun."
She left to find her friends, then there were none.

*(continued on next page)*

NAME                                                                                    | DATE

## Butterfly Countdown page 3 of 5

*(continued on next page)*

**NAME** | **DATE**

## Butterfly Countdown page 4 of 5

Use the numbers to help solve the problems below.

0   1   2   3   4   5   6   7   8   9   10

Solve the addition problems. Use the pictures to help.

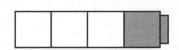

3 + 1 = _____

2 + 1 = _____

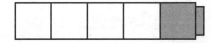

4 + 1 = _____

1 + 1 = _____

7 + 1 = _____

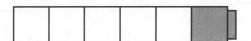

5 + 1 = _____

8 + 1 = _____

*(continued on next page)*

NAME | DATE

## Butterfly Countdown page 5 of 5

Solve the subtraction problems. Use the pictures to help.

10 – 1 = _____

8 – 1 = _____

4 – 1 = _____

6 – 1 = _____

7 – 1 = _____

2 – 1 = _____

## Add a Circle & Subtract a Spider page 1 of 2

## Add a Circle

Trace the numbers and complete the addition problems below. Use the pictures to help.

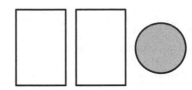 2 + 1 = 3

____

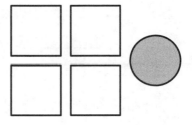 4 + 1 = 5

____

 6 + 1 = 7

____

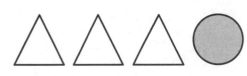 3 + 1 =

____

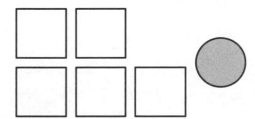 5 + 1 =

____

NAME | DATE

## Add a Circle & Subtract a Spider page 2 of 2

## Subtract a Spider

Trace the numbers and complete the subtraction problems below. Use the pictures to help.

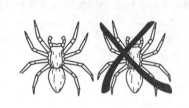

$$2 - 1 = 1$$

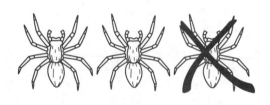

$$3 - 1 = 2$$

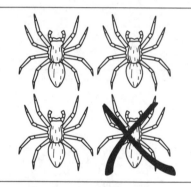

$$4 - 1 =$$

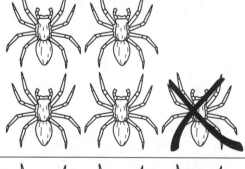

$$5 - 1 =$$

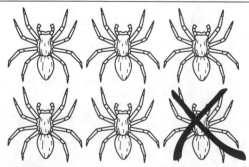

$$6 - 1 =$$

**64**

**Bikes & Trikes** page 1 of 2

**1** Draw a line from each numeral to the matching ten-frame. One has been done for you as an example.

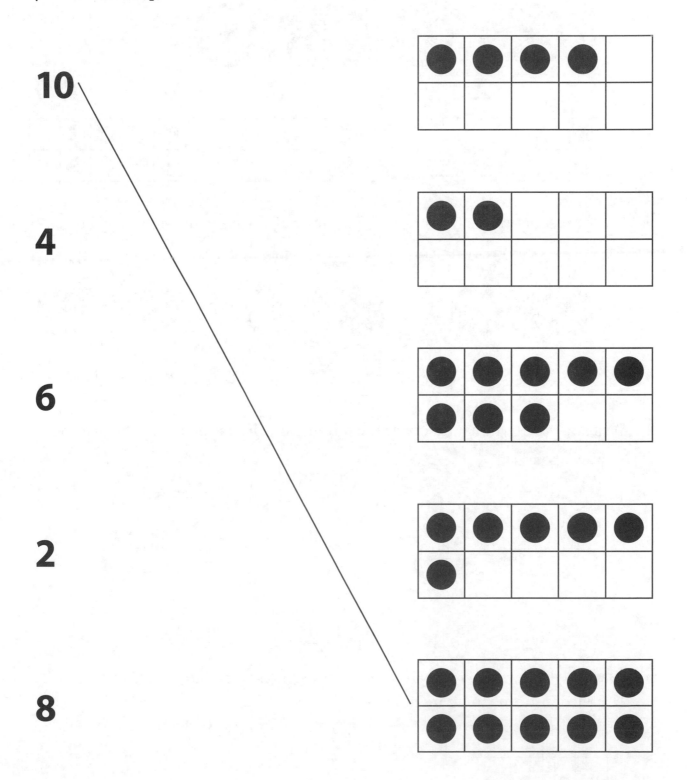

(continued on next page)

NAME | DATE

## Bikes & Trikes  page 2 of 2

**2**  Circle the ten-frame that shows the number of **wheels** you see in the picture.

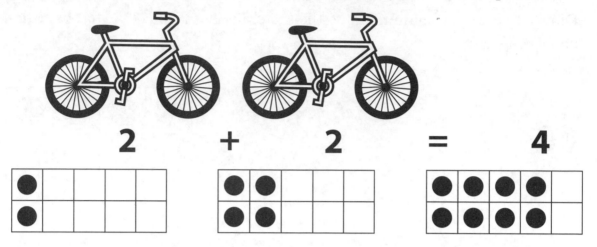

2     +     2     =     4

**3**  Write an equation that describes the number of **wheels** you see in the picture.

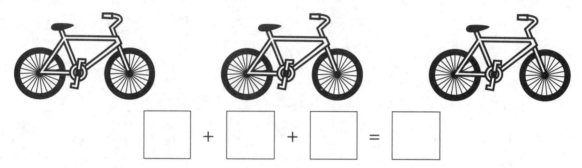

☐ + ☐ + ☐ = ☐

**4**  Write an equation that describes the number of **wheels** you see in the picture.

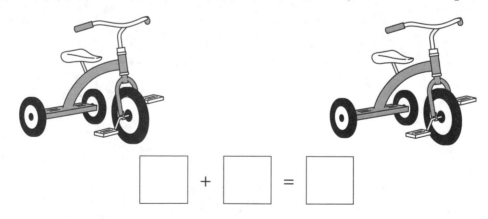

☐ + ☐ = ☐

**5**  <u>CHALLENGE</u>  How many **wheels** would you see on 2 bikes and 1 trike?
Use the ten-frame to figure it out.

66

NAME

DATE

 **Count & Compare** page 1 of 2

## Which One Has More Dots?

Put an X on the domino that has more dots. Trace the numbers below.

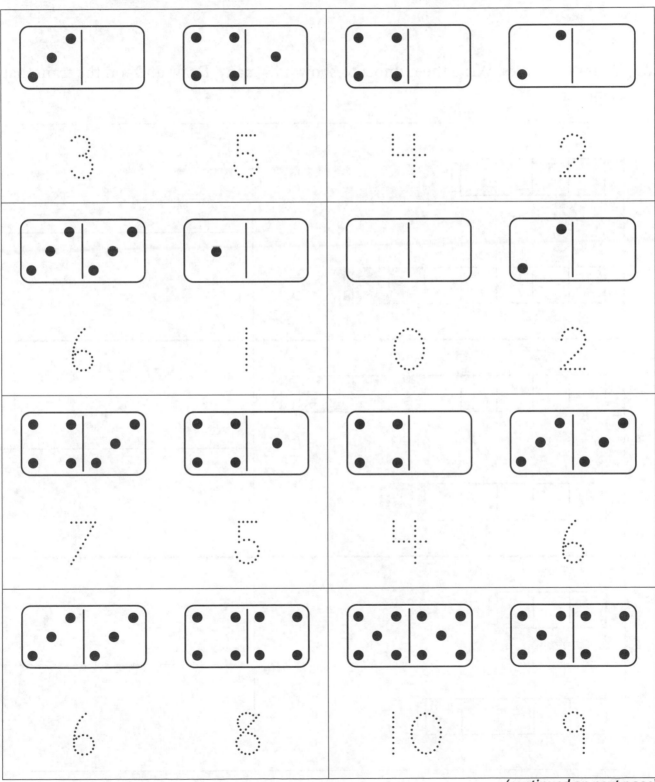

*(continued on next page)*

**NAME** | **DATE**

## Count & Compare page 2 of 2

**1** Trace the numbers.

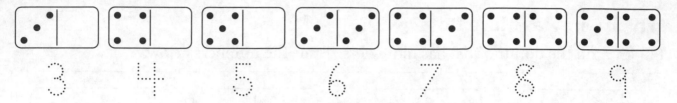

3    4    5    6    7    8    9

**2** Count the cubes. Write the number to show how many. Draw an X on the train that is longer.

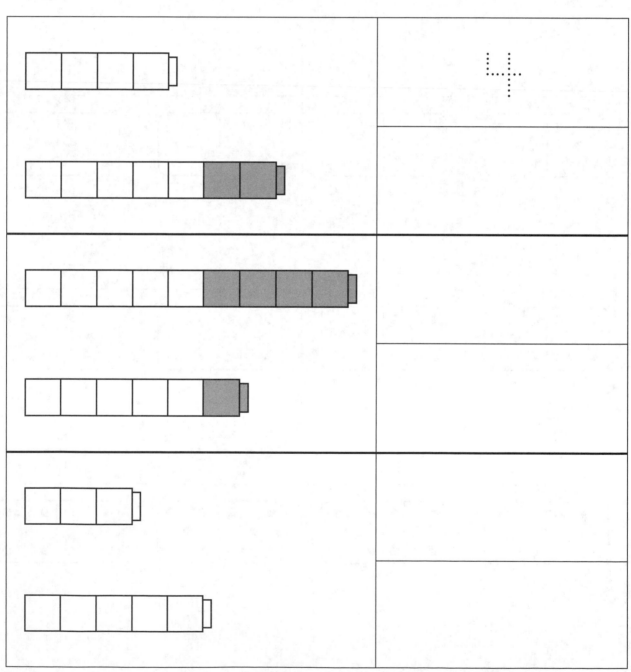

NAME | DATE

 **Numbers & Ten-Frames Bingo** page 1 of 3

### Note to Families

Your child can practice ordering ten-frames and matching numbers in this bingo game. You can help by having your child put the game cards in order before and after you play the game.

## Materials

- Numbers & Ten-Frames Bingo, pages 1–3
- game markers (such as pennies, cereal pieces, dry beans, small pieces of paper)

## Instructions

**1** Cut apart the bingo boards on page 2 and the bingo cards on page 3.

**2** Set out the cards in order from 2 to 10. Then mix them up and put them in a pile face-down.

**3** Decide which bingo board you each will use.

**4** Take turns turning over a card and saying the number. Both players look for the number on their bingo boards and cover it with a game marker.

**5** The first player to get three in a row in any direction is the winner!

**6** Play again, and save the cards to play another day.

**7** When you are done, put the cards in order again.

**8** **CHALLENGE** If your child is comfortable putting the cards in order, try it going backward from 10 to 2.

*(continued on next page)*

**Numbers & Ten-Frames Bingo** page 2 of 3

| 6 | 3 | 4 |
|---|---|---|
| 2 | 8 | 9 |
| 10 | 7 | 5 |

(continued on next page)

| 5 | 9 | 2 |
|---|---|---|
| 4 | 10 | 7 |
| 8 | 6 | 3 |

72

NAME | DATE

## Numbers & Ten-Frames Bingo page 3 of 3

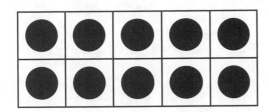
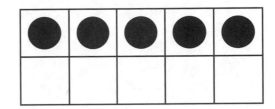

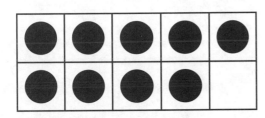
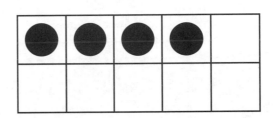

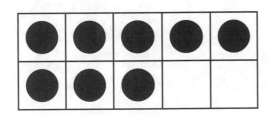
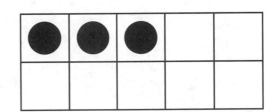

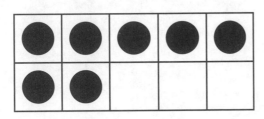

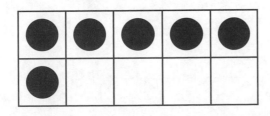

NAME _____ | DATE _____

 **What Comes Next?** page 1 of 2

## What Comes Next?

**1** Draw or color what you think comes next in the pattern.

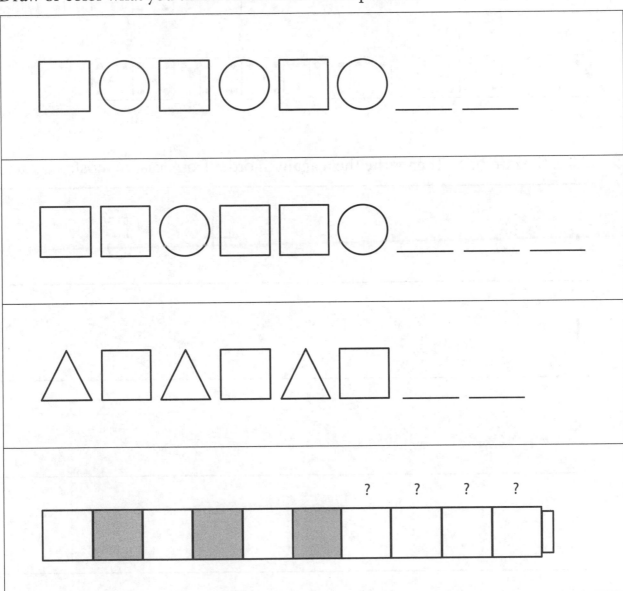

**2** Fill in the numbers that are missing.

| 1 | | 3 | 4 | 5 | | 7 | 8 | | 10 |
|---|---|---|---|---|---|---|---|---|---|

NAME | DATE

## What Comes Next?  page 2 of 2

## Put Them in Order

Use the numbers and dominoes to help with the problems below.

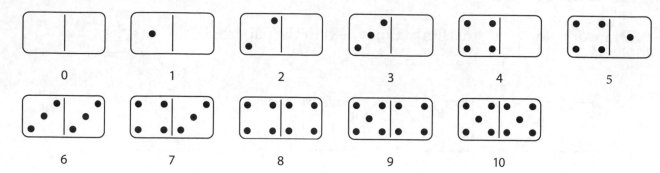

**3**  Trace the numbers. Then write them again in order from least to most.

| | | | | | | |
|---|---|---|---|---|---|---|
| **a** | 5 | 6 | 4 | 4 | 5 | 6 |
| **b** | 8 | 6 | 7 | | | |
| **c** | 4 | 2 | 3 | | | |
| **d** | 3 | 1 | 2 | | | |
| **e** | 10 | 8 | 9 | | | |
| **f** | 7 | 9 | 8 | | | |

76

**Double It!** page 1 of 4

**Note to Families**

This game, which we have been playing in school, will help your child learn counting by 2s and doubles facts.

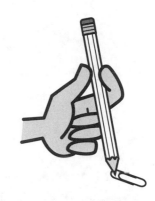

## Materials

- Double It! pages 1–4
- 10 counters (pennies, cereal pieces, dried beans, etc.)
- game marker for each player (any small object)
- paperclip and pencil (for spinner)

## Instructions

**1** As a warm-up, use the 10 counters and ask your child how much is 1 counter and 1 more, 2 counters and 2 more, and so on.

- Place one pair at a time on the ten-frame on page 2, starting at the left, and talk about how the doubled numbers are even—they always make perfect pairs with no "leftovers."

- With all 10 counters on the ten-frame, model counting by 2s: "2, 4, 6, 8, 10," and then "10, 8, 6, 4, 2."

**2** To play the game, take turns spinning, using the spinner on page 2, and doubling the number. To help with doubling, use the dominoes at the bottom of the game board (page 3) or the counting materials.

**ex** Spin 2, double it to 4. Spin 5, double it to 10.

**3** Check to see if the doubled number is on the next wheel on the game board. If it is, move your bicycle (marker) to that circle.

**4** The first one to get to the last (5th) wheel is the winner.

**5** Play again going backward, from the 5th wheel back to the 1st.

**6** Complete the worksheet on page 4 and return it to your teacher.

*(continued on next page)*

NAME | DATE

## Double It! page 2 of 4

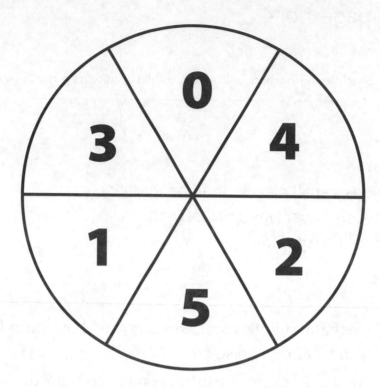

## Ten-Frame

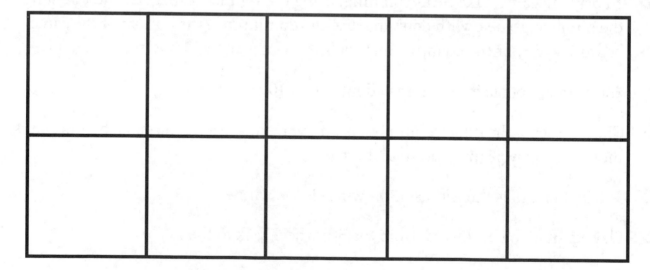

*(continued on next page)*

NAME

DATE

## Double It! page 3 of 4

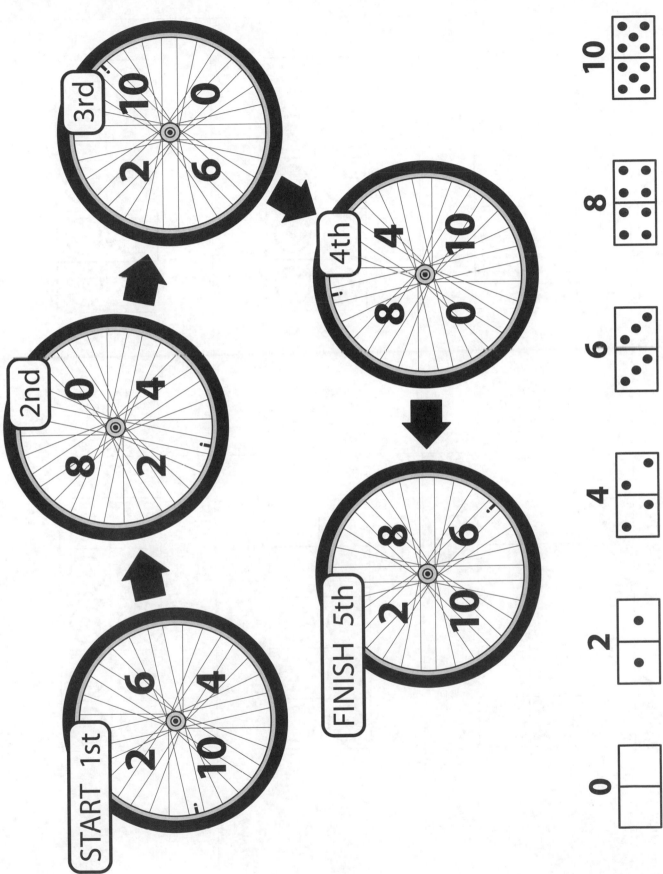

*(continued on next page)*

NAME

DATE

## Double It! page 4 of 4

Solve the addition problems. Use the pictures to help.

$$
\begin{array}{r}
2 \\
+2 \\
\hline
\end{array}
$$

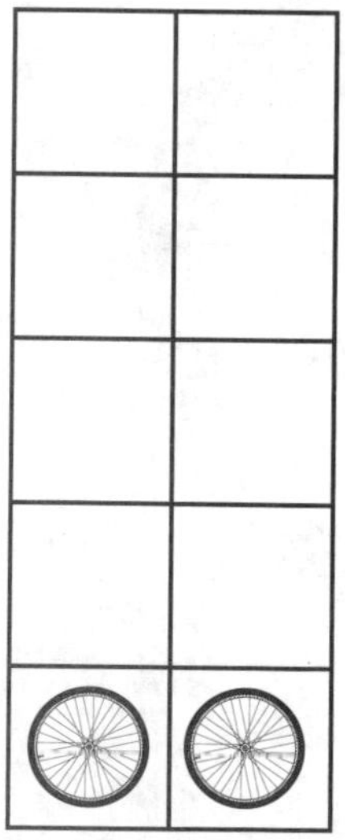

$$
\begin{array}{r}
4 \\
+4 \\
\hline
\end{array}
$$

$$
\begin{array}{r}
5 \\
+5 \\
\hline
\end{array}
$$

$$
\begin{array}{r}
1 \\
+1 \\
\hline 2
\end{array}
$$

$$
\begin{array}{r}
3 \\
+3 \\
\hline
\end{array}
$$

$$
\begin{array}{r}
4 \\
+4 \\
\hline
\end{array}
$$

**NAME** _____ | **DATE** _____

## 🏠 **Ordering & Comparing Numbers** page 1 of 2

**1** Trace each number. Then write it again in the box below.

| 0 | 1 | 2 | 3 | 4 | 5 | 6 | 7 | 8 | 9 | 10 |
|---|---|---|---|---|---|---|---|---|---|----|
|   |   |   |   |   |   |   |   |   |   |    |

**2** Fill in the missing numbers on the number line below.

0    1    2    3    4         6

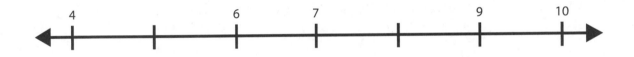

4         6    7         9    10

**3** **CHALLENGE**

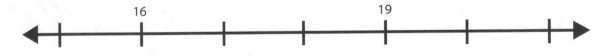

16              19

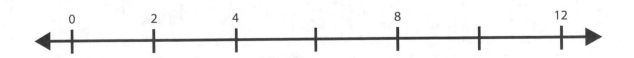

0    2    4         8              12

*(continued on next page)*

## Ordering & Comparing Numbers page 2 of 2

**4** Fill in the missing numbers in the cards below.

| 0 | | 2 | | | 6 | | 9 | |

**a** On the number line, circle the numbers greater than 7.

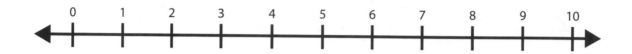

**b** On the number line, circle the numbers less than 4.

**c** On the number line, circle the number between 6 and 8.

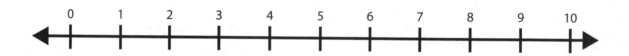

**d** On the number line, circle the number that is 1 more than 5.

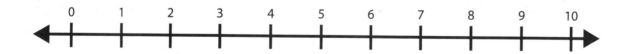

**5** **CHALLENGE** Fill in the missing numbers in the cards below.

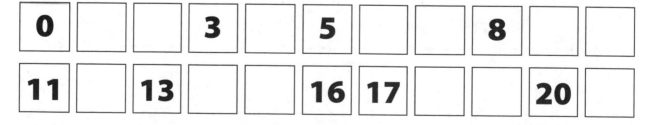

| 0 | | | 3 | | 5 | | | 8 | | |
| 11 | | 13 | | | 16 | 17 | | | 20 | |

**Fours & Fives** page 1 of 2

## Note to Families

Help your child "count on" instead of counting from 1 every time. For example, if there are three dots on the first hand and two on the second, say "3, 4, 5!"

**1** Color the cubes to match each equation.

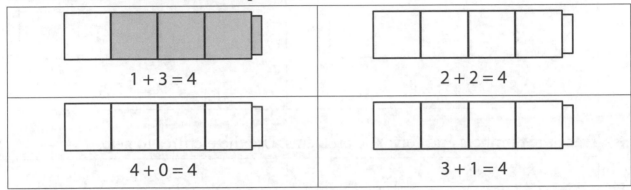

$1 + 3 = 4$          $2 + 2 = 4$

$4 + 0 = 4$          $3 + 1 = 4$

**2** Trace the numbers and solve the problems. Use the pictures to help.

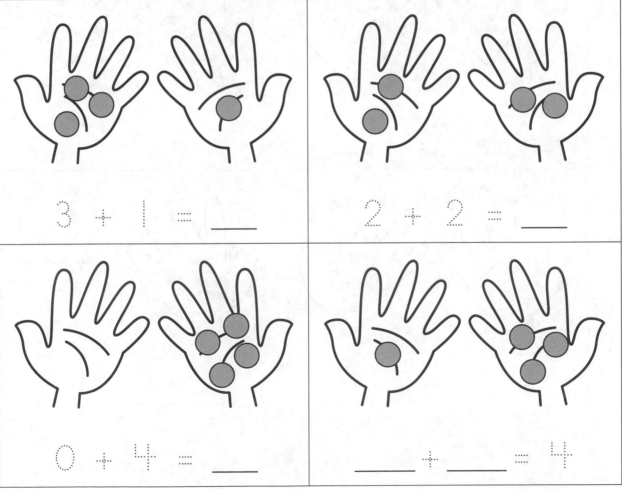

$3 + 1 = \underline{\phantom{0}}$        $2 + 2 = \underline{\phantom{0}}$

$0 + 4 = \underline{\phantom{0}}$        $\underline{\phantom{0}} + \underline{\phantom{0}} = 4$

*(continued on next page)*

NAME | DATE

## Fours & Fives page 2 of 2

**3** Color the cubes to match each equation.

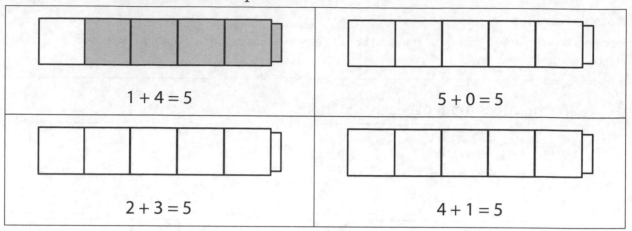

$1 + 4 = 5$

$5 + 0 = 5$

$2 + 3 = 5$

$4 + 1 = 5$

**4** Trace the numbers and solve the problems. Use the pictures to help.

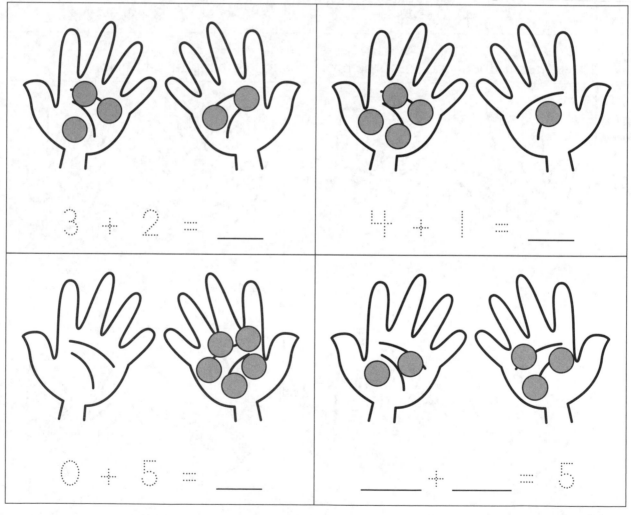

$3 + 2 = \underline{\hspace{1cm}}$

$4 + 1 = \underline{\hspace{1cm}}$

$0 + 5 = \underline{\hspace{1cm}}$

$\underline{\hspace{1cm}} + \underline{\hspace{1cm}} = 5$

**NAME** | **DATE**

 **The Forest Game** page 1 of 4

### Note to Families

This game will help your child practice adding and subtracting by following the directions on the spinner. Your child may recognize the words *Add* and *Subtract* on the spinner; if not, help read the words and the signs (+ and –) that go with them.

## Materials

- The Forest Game, pages 1–4
- paperclip and pencil (for spinning)
- 20 game markers (pennies, cereal pieces, dry beans, etc.)

## Instructions

**1** Each player needs a game board (pages 3 and 4) and 10 game markers—these will be your squirrels.

**2** Set up your boards with 5 squirrels on the first 5 nuts, and another 5 squirrels off to the side for each player.

**3** Look at the spinner before you start playing. Talk about what the words and signs mean.

**4** Take turns spinning the spinner. Follow the directions on the spinner.

- Your squirrels will hop in and out of the forest depending on the spinner directions.
- If the spinner says *Add*, add that number of squirrels to your board. How many squirrels are in your forest now? How many more do you need to get to 10?
- If the spinner says *Subtract*, hop that number of squirrels off your board (and out of the forest). How many squirrels are in your forest now? How many more do you need to get to 10?

**5** Take turns spinning, adding or subtracting squirrels, and reporting the results until one player has collected exactly 10 squirrels in the forest. That player wins the game.

**6** Complete the worksheet (page 2) and return the paper to your teacher.

*(continued on next page)*

NAME _____ | DATE _____

## The Forest Game page 2 of 4

**1** What did you think of The Forest Game? Talk about it together. Think about these questions. Ask an adult to write down your answers.

> **a** What did you like about it?

> **b** What did you learn?

> **c** Were you counting by 1s, counting on, or did you just "see" how many squirrels you had in the forest?

**2** Solve some Squirrels & Nuts problems. Help the squirrels get some nuts by adding and subtracting.

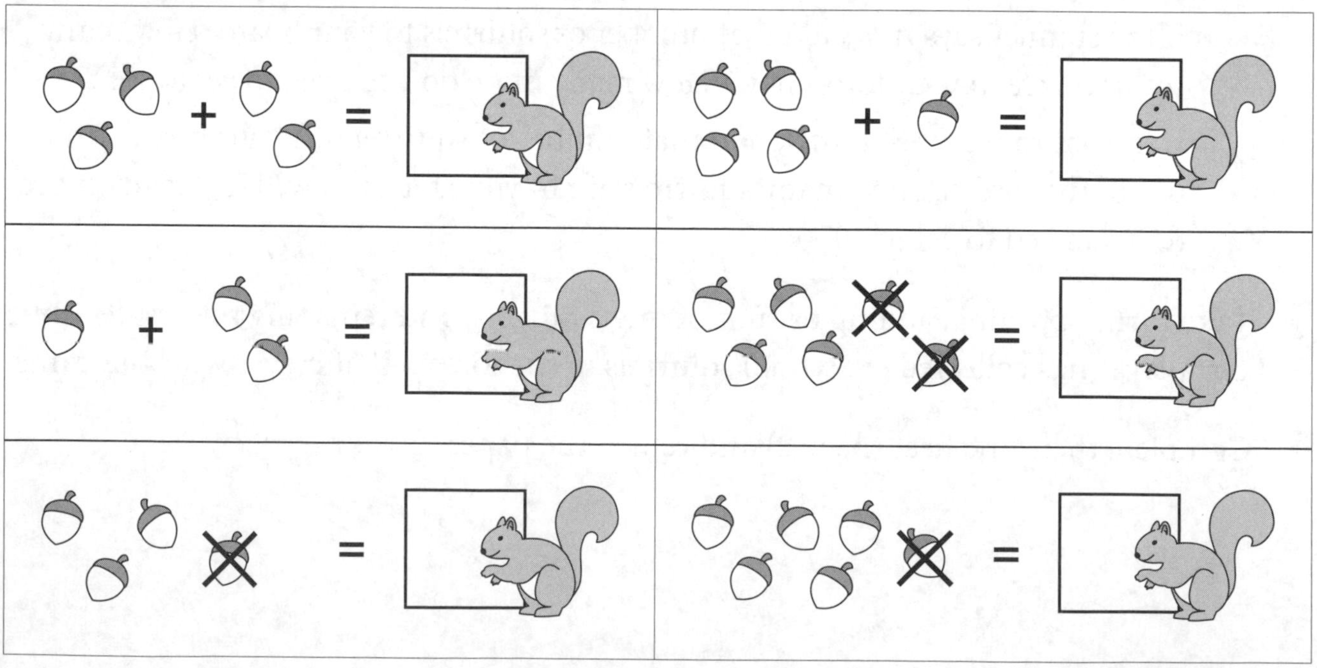

*(continued on next page)*

86

NAME

DATE

## The Forest Game page 3 of 4

*(continued on next page)*

NAME | DATE

## The Forest Game page 4 of 4

NAME | DATE

 **Longer & Shorter, More & Less** page 1 of 2

**1** Draw a red X on the longer pencil. Color the shorter pencil green.

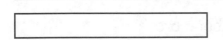

**2** Color the longer vehicle yellow. Draw a circle around the shorter vehicle.

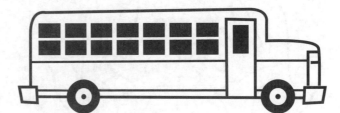

**3** Color the longest ribbon blue. Color the shortest ribbon red.

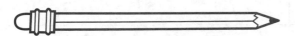

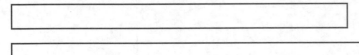

*(continued on next page)*

**NAME** _____ | **DATE** _____

## Longer & Shorter, More & Less page 2 of 2

**4** How many pennies are there in each hand? Write the number to show. Draw a blue X on the hand in each box with fewer pennies.

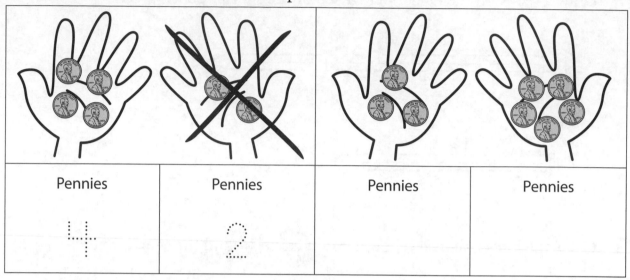

| Pennies | Pennies | Pennies | Pennies |
| 4 | 2 | | |

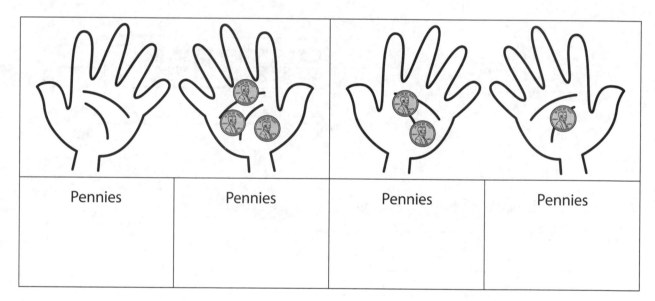

| Pennies | Pennies | Pennies | Pennies |

**5** Color the longest ribbon green. Color the shortest ribbon brown.

NAME | DATE

## 🏠 Frogs & More Frogs page 1 of 2

**1** Freddy Frog is practicing for the big frog jump contest. Color in the boxes to show how far he jumped each time.

1st Jump: 8 sticks

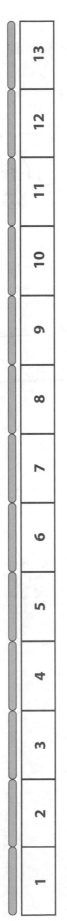

| 1 | 2 | 3 | 4 | 5 | 6 | 7 | 8 | 9 | 10 | 11 | 12 | 13 |

2nd Jump: 12 sticks

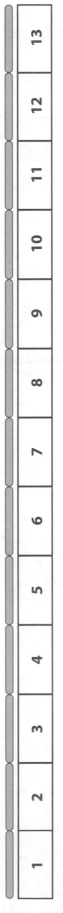

| 1 | 2 | 3 | 4 | 5 | 6 | 7 | 8 | 9 | 10 | 11 | 12 | 13 |

3rd Jump: 9 sticks

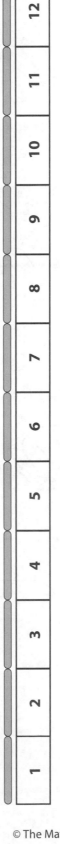

| 1 | 2 | 3 | 4 | 5 | 6 | 7 | 8 | 9 | 10 | 11 | 12 | 13 |

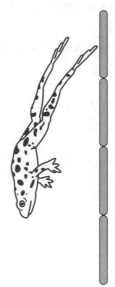

**2** Which one was his longest jump? (Circle one.)

8 sticks          12 sticks          9 sticks

**3** Which one was his shortest jump? (Circle one.)

8 sticks          12 sticks          9 sticks

(continued on next page)

**NAME** _____ | **DATE** _____

## Frogs & More Frogs  page 2 of 2

**4**  Color the frogs. Trace the numbers or symbols. Write an addition sentence to match the picture.

Color 2 frogs green. Color 3 frogs brown.

2 + 3 = _____

Color 4 frogs red. Color 1 frog blue.

_____ + _____ = _____

Color 3 frogs yellow. Color 2 frogs black.

_____ + _____ = _____

**5**  Add.

| 1 | 3 | 4 | 2 | 3 | 4 |
|---|---|---|---|---|---|
| + 2 | + 1 | + 1 | +2 | + 2 | + 2 |

**94**

**NAME** | **DATE**

 **Comparing Pennies** page 1 of 2

**1** Count the pennies in each frame. Write how many there are. Then draw lines to the words to show which frame has more and which has less.

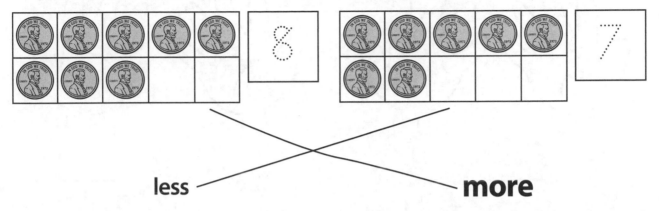

less          **more**

**2**

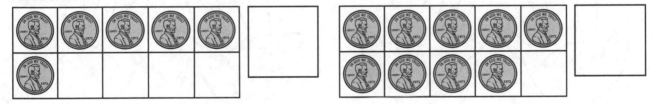

less          **more**

**3**

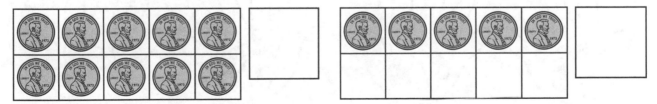

less          **more**

*(continued on next page)*

**NAME** | **DATE**

## Comparing Pennies page 2 of 2

**4** How many pennies are there in each hand? Write the number to show. Draw a blue X on the hand with fewer pennies.

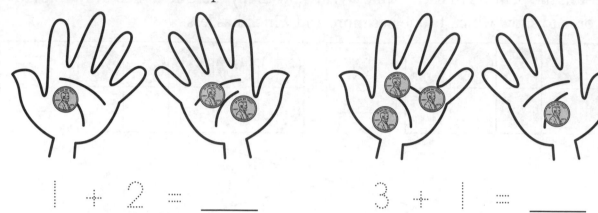

1 + 2 = _____          3 + 1 = _____

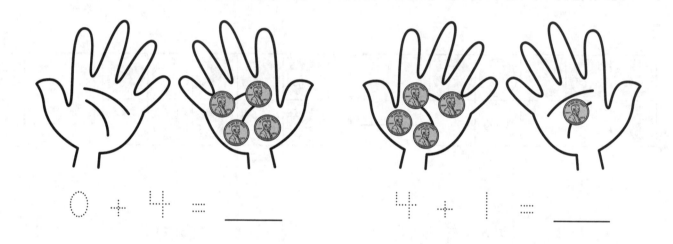

0 + 4 = _____          4 + 1 = _____

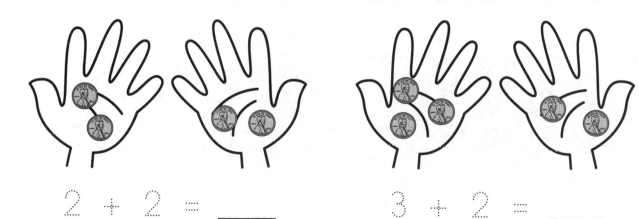

2 + 2 = _____          3 + 2 = _____

**96**

**NAME** _____ | **DATE** _____

## 🏠 **Adding Pennies** page 1 of 2

Solve the addition problems. Use the pictures to help.

$$2¢ + 3¢ = \underline{\hspace{2cm}}¢$$

$$3¢ + 2¢ = \underline{\hspace{2cm}}¢$$

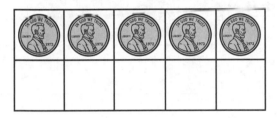

$$5¢ + 0¢ = \underline{\hspace{2cm}}¢$$

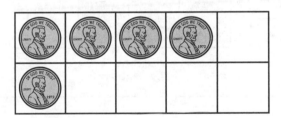

$$4¢ + 1¢ = \underline{\hspace{2cm}}¢$$

$$1¢ + 4¢ = \underline{\hspace{2cm}}¢$$

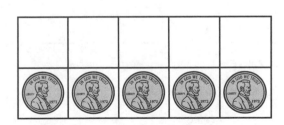

$$0¢ + 5¢ = \underline{\hspace{2cm}}¢$$

*(continued on next page)*

NAME _____ | DATE _____

## Adding Pennies page 2 of 2

Solve the addition problems. Use the pictures to help.

$$\begin{array}{r} 1 \\ +1 \\ \hline \end{array}$$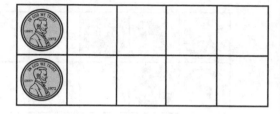

$$\begin{array}{r} 2 \\ +2 \\ \hline \end{array}$$

$$\begin{array}{r} 3 \\ +3 \\ \hline \end{array}$$

$$\begin{array}{r} 4 \\ +4 \\ \hline \end{array}$$

$$\begin{array}{r} 4 \\ +4 \\ \hline \end{array}$$

$$\begin{array}{r} 5 \\ +5 \\ \hline \end{array}$$

**CHALLENGE**

5 + 4 = _____ ¢          5 + 3 = _____ ¢

# Money March & Search for Circles page 1 of 3

## Note to Families

In this game, which we have already played in school, your child will review the names and values of pennies and nickels, counting money, and thinking in terms of "5 and some more."

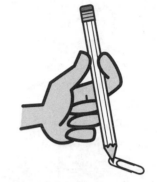

## Materials

- Money March & Search For Circles pages 1–3
- pencil and paperclip (for a spinner)
- 2 different game markers (such as a bean and a button)

## Instructions

**1** Before you play, talk about the coins on the game board and spinner on page 2 (pennies and nickels) and how much they are worth (1¢ and 5¢).

**2** During the game, help your child when necessary to identify the coins and figure out how much they are worth. Encourage counting on from 5.

**3** Take turns spinning the spinner.

- Say the coins that you spin and the number of each.
  For example, "I got one nickel and one penny."

- Figure out how much your coins are worth.
  For example, "That's 5 and 1 more—6!"

- Move your "horse" (game marker) along the path that many spaces.
  For example, "I get to move 6—1, 2, 3, 4, 5, 6."

**4** Keep playing until one player gets a horse (marker) all the way to the barn.

**5** **CHALLENGE** After you spin the spinner and determine the amount, roll a die and add that much more. Advance that number on the path. For an even greater challenge, spin twice and add the two amounts together; then advance that far on the path.

**6** Complete the worksheet on page 3 and return it to your teacher.

*(continued on next page)*

 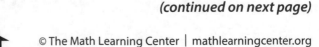 **99**

**100**

NAME | DATE

# Money March & Search for Circles page 2 of 3

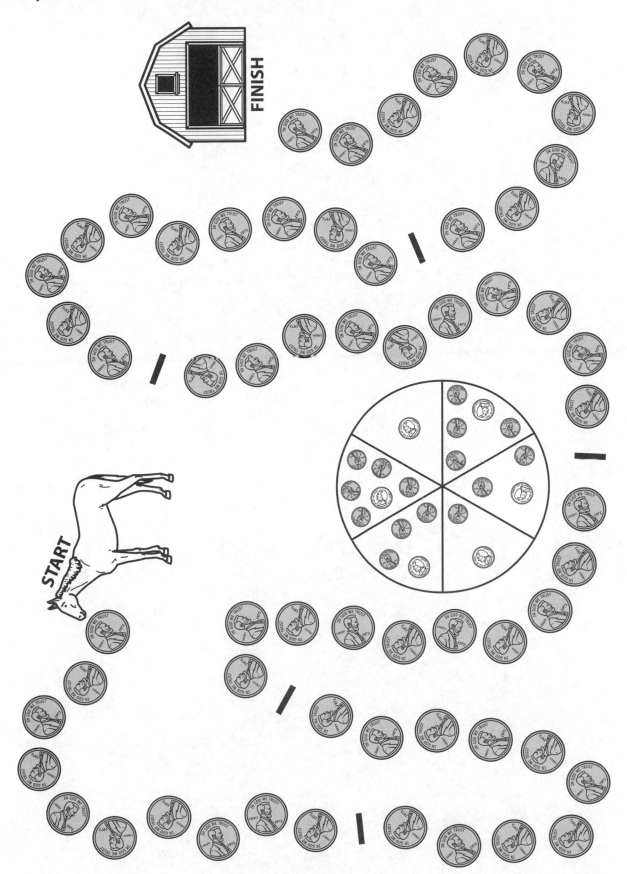

*(continued on next page)*

  **101** © The Math Learning Center | mathlearningcenter.org

102

## Money March & Search for Circles page 3 of 3

Circles are all around us! Search all over your house for things with a circle shape—a clock or checkers, for example. Draw an item in a box (one clock in one box, one checker in another, for example), count how many you find, and write the number on the line. If there are too many to count, you could say "lots" or leave it blank.

| | | | |
|---|---|---|---|
| **How many?** | **How many?** | **How many?** | **How many?** |
| **How many?** | **How many?** | **How many?** | **How many?** |
| **How many?** | **How many?** | **How many?** | **How many?** |

NAME _____ | DATE _____

 **Race You to 15¢** page 1 of 3

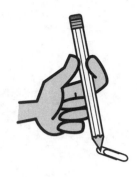

## Materials

- Race You to 15¢ pages 1–3
- pencil and paperclip (for a spinner)
- 12 pennies and 5 nickels (if you don't have these coins available, use any type of game markers, one kind for pennies and another kind for nickels)

## Instructions

**1** As you play this game, be sure to wait until your partner has finished a turn (spinning, counting, and trading) before you have your turn.

**2** Take turns spinning the spinner. How many pennies do you get? Count them out on the board.

**3** If there are more than 5 pennies, set any extras to the side for a minute. Trade 5 pennies in for a nickel and then move any extra pennies onto the penny strip. How much money do you have all together?

**4** Continue taking turns spinning and collecting pennies and nickels until one player has exactly 3 nickels (15¢). If you spin a number that's more than what you need to have 15¢ exactly, you need to wait for your next turn to try again.

**5** **CHALLENGE** Spin the spinner twice and add the two amounts together. Play as usual.

**6** Complete the worksheet on page 3 and return it to your teacher.

*(continued on next page)*

**NAME** _____ | **DATE** _____

## Race You to 15¢ page 2 of 3

**15¢**

nickels

pennies

**Player 1**

**15¢**

nickels

pennies

**Player 2**

1 2 3 **5** 4 6 7 8 9 **10** 11 12 13 14 **15**

*(continued on next page)*

NAME _____ | DATE _____

## Race You to 15¢ page 3 of 3

**1** Color the cubes to match the equation.

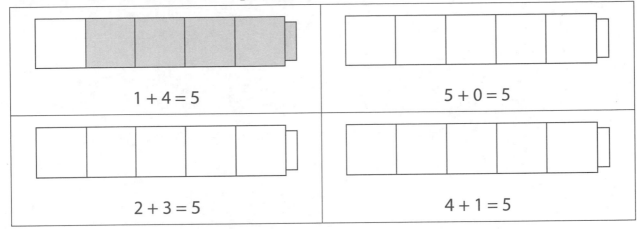

$1 + 4 = 5$

$5 + 0 = 5$

$2 + 3 = 5$

$4 + 1 = 5$

**2** Trace the numbers and solve the problems. Use the pictures to help.

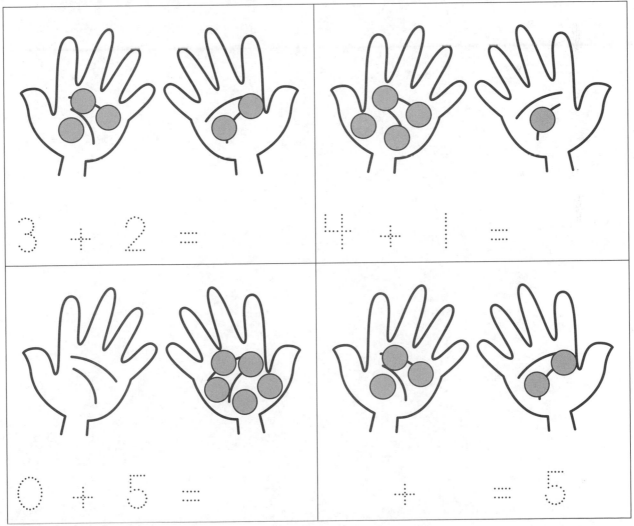

$3 + 2 =$

$4 + 1 =$

$0 + 5 =$

$+ = 5$

NAME _____ | DATE _____

 **Shape Bingo** page 1 of 4

### Note to Families

This activity will help your child practice shape names while looking for ways in which triangles, squares, circles, and rectangles are alike and different.

## Materials

- Shape Bingo, pages 1–4
- 15–20 game markers (such as dry beans, buttons, Lego pieces, etc.)
- scissors
- envelope

## Instructions

**1** Cut apart the shape attribute cards on page 3 and put them in an envelope.

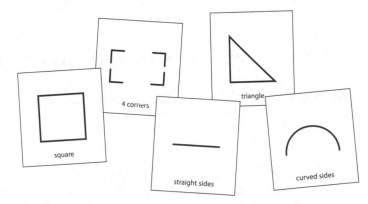

**2** Cut apart the two bingo boards on page 4 and give one to each player, along with half the game markers.

**3** Pull a card out of the envelope.

- What does the card show?
- Do you have a shape on your game board that matches the card?
- Does your partner have one?
- Did you make the same choice as your partner or a different choice?

**4** On each turn, players cover just one shape on their game boards, even if more than one shape matches the card.

*(continued on next page)*

NAME                                                                    | DATE

**Shape Bingo** page 2 of 4

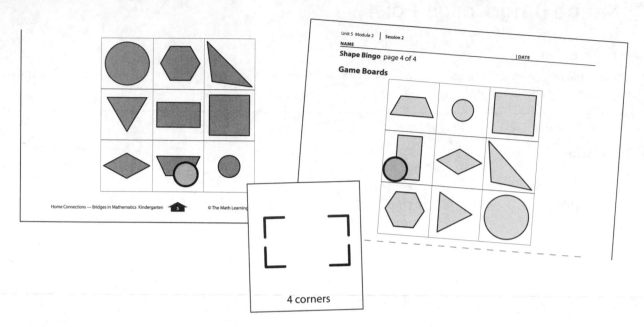

4 corners

**5** Take turns pulling cards out of the envelope and finding shapes on your boards that match.

**6** The first player to get three markers in a row in any direction wins the game.

**7** Save the game boards and the envelope of cards and play again a few times this week.

*(continued on next page)*

## Shape Bingo page 3 of 4

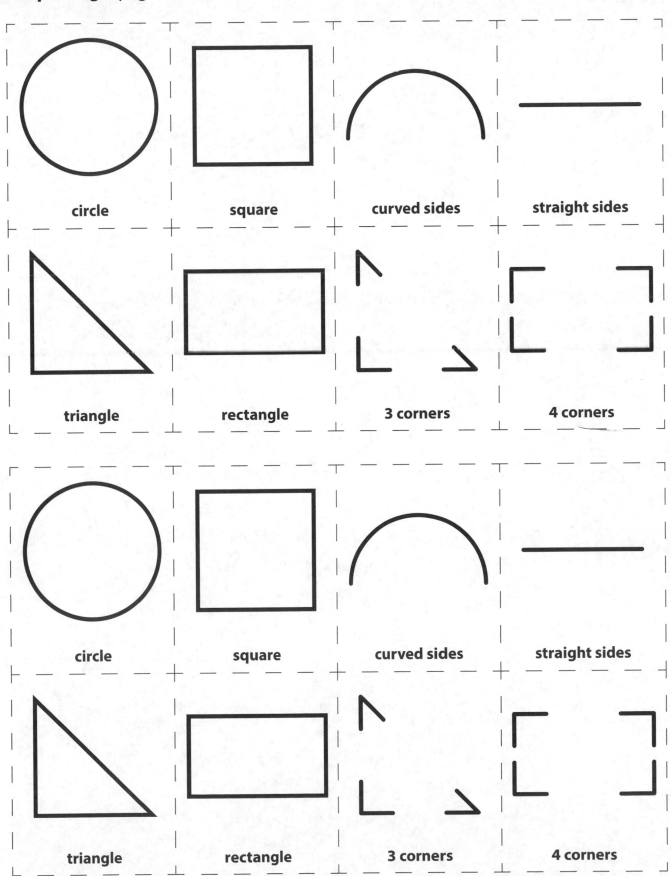

circle

square

curved sides

straight sides

triangle

rectangle

3 corners

4 corners

circle

square

curved sides

straight sides

triangle

rectangle

3 corners

4 corners

*(continued on next page)*

## Shape Bingo page 4 of 4

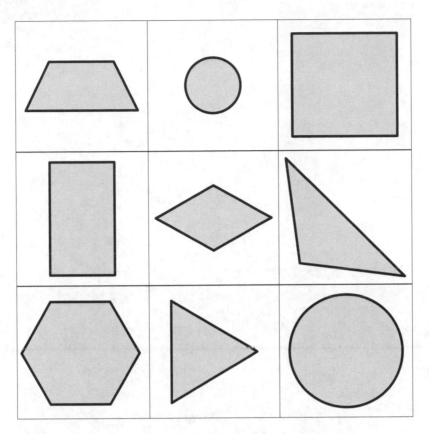

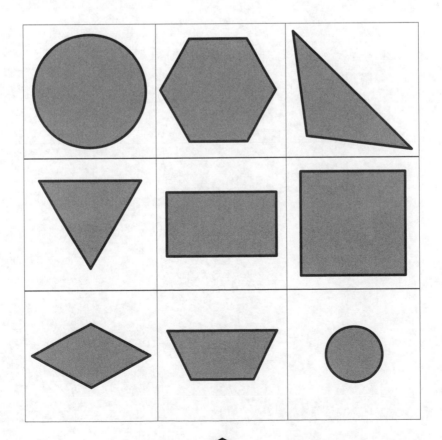

NAME | DATE

 **Shape Sorting & Patterning** page 1 of 5

### Note to Families

The whole family can get involved in this Home Connection by helping to color and cut the shapes.

## Materials

- Shape Sorting & Patterning, pages 1–5
- red, yellow, and blue crayons
- scissors
- envelope

## Instructions

**1** Work together to color each of the shapes on pages 3–5. Use the color specified on each page.

**2** Cut around the boxes and keep the cards in an envelope.

**3** Find different ways to sort the shapes: by color, size, type, number of sides, number of corners, or by curved or straight sides.

These are big.

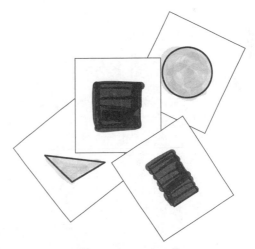

These are small.

**4** Ask someone to guess how you sorted the shapes.

*(continued on next page)*

**NAME** _____ | **DATE** _____

## Shape Sorting & Patterning page 2 of 5

**5** On another day, make some patterns using your shapes.

circle     square     triangle     circle     square     triangle

**6** Ask someone to figure out your pattern. What would come next?

**7** Make sure to label and save the envelope of shape cards.

**8** <u>CHALLENGE</u> Make a "tricky" pattern!

*(continued on next page)*

## Shape Sorting & Patterning page 3 of 5

Color each shape yellow.

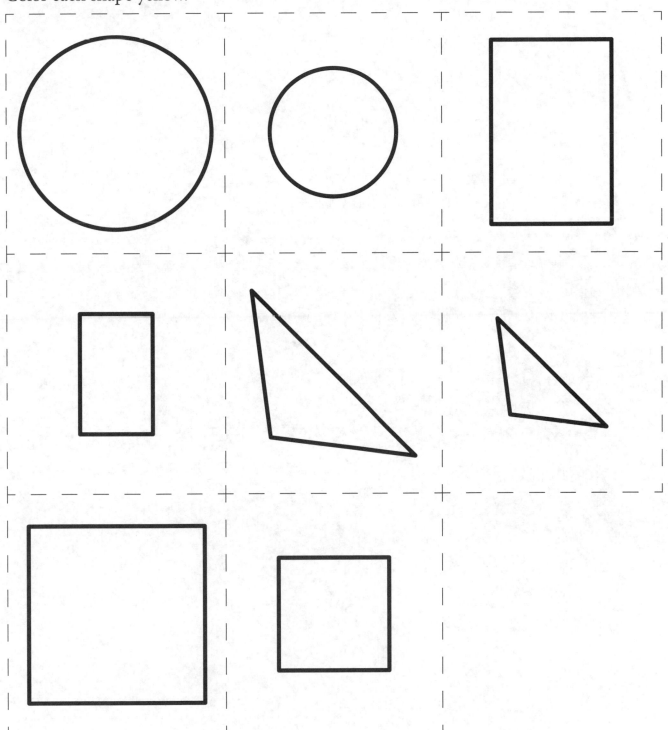

*(continued on next page)*

119

**NAME** | **DATE**

## Shape Sorting & Patterning page 4 of 5

Color each shape red.

*(continued on next page)*

121

NAME

DATE

## Shape Sorting & Patterning page 5 of 5

Color each shape blue.

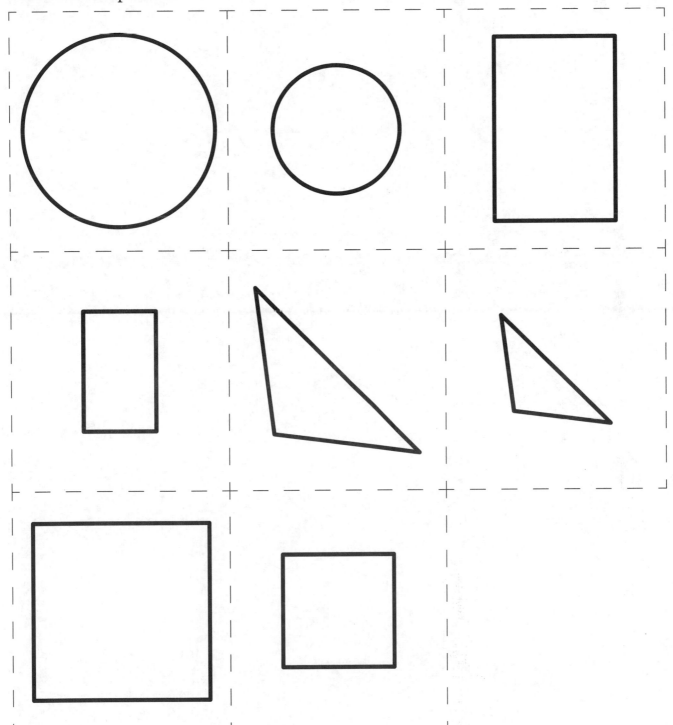

NAME | DATE

 **Pattern Block Puzzles** page 1 of 4

## Note to Families
Adult help will be needed for cutting out the pattern block shapes. You will probably only need about half of each shape, and you may have some left over from Pattern Block Butterflies. Remind your child to flip and turn the paper shapes to get them to fit.

## Materials
- Pattern Blocks Puzzles, pages 1–4
- pattern block paper shapes (yellow hexagons, red trapezoids, green triangles, blue rhombuses, orange squares, and white rhombuses; sent home from school)
- scissors
- glue
- an envelope (to save the leftover pattern block paper shapes)

## Instructions

**1** Ask someone to help you cut out the pattern block paper shapes. You will probably only need about half of each shape. Do you have any left from Pattern Block Butterflies?

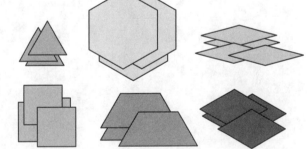

**2** Find a way to fill the first tugboat with pattern block paper shapes. To make the pieces fit within the lines, you might have to flip or turn pieces.

**3** When the tugboat is filled in, glue the shapes down.

**4** Now try the same thing with the first helicopter. Fit the pieces and glue them down.

**5** After you've done both puzzles, see if you can find a new way to fill in each of them. Glue the new pieces on the second tugboat and helicopter.

**6** Complete the How Many Pieces? worksheet, and return it to your teacher.

**7** **CHALLENGE** Make your own design and glue it on a piece of paper.

*(continued on next page)*

NAME

| DATE

## Pattern Block Puzzles page 2 of 4

## Tugboats

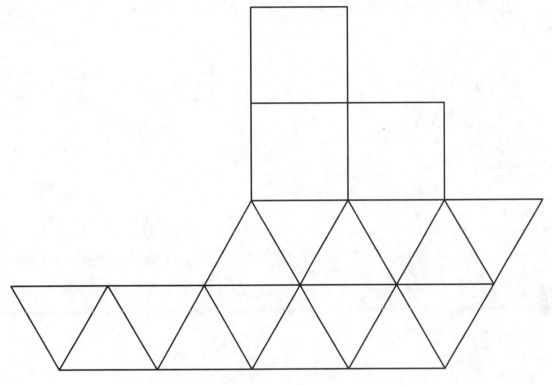

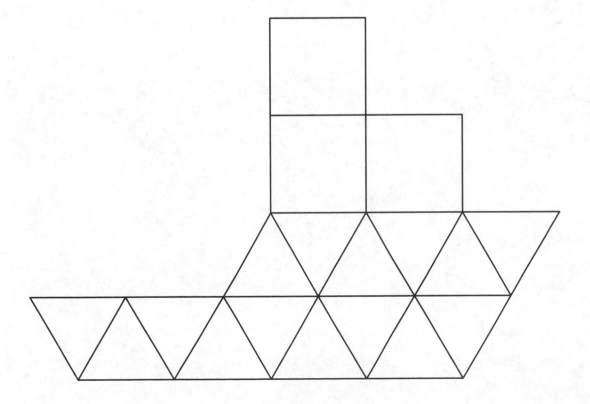

*(continued on next page)*

## Pattern Block Puzzles page 3 of 4

## Helicopters

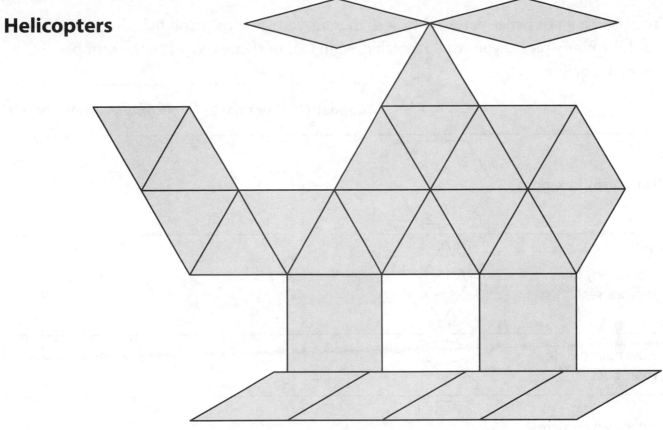

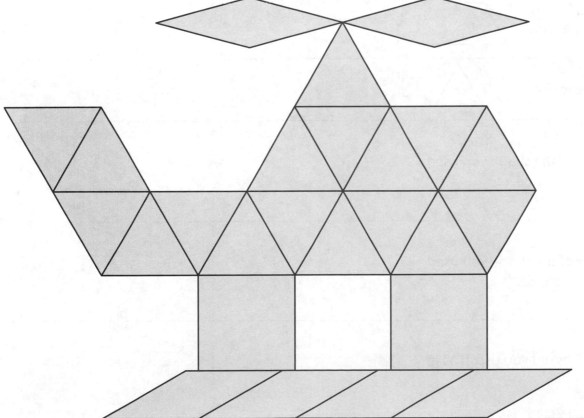

(continued on next page)

**NAME** | **DATE**

## Pattern Block Puzzles page 4 of 4

You used a lot of paper pattern block shapes for your tugboats and helicopters. Let's find out how many pieces you used in each design! Count them and write the numbers in the chart below.

|  | Tugboat 1 | Tugboat 2 | Helicopter 1 | Helicopter 2 |
|---|---|---|---|---|
| How many hexagons? 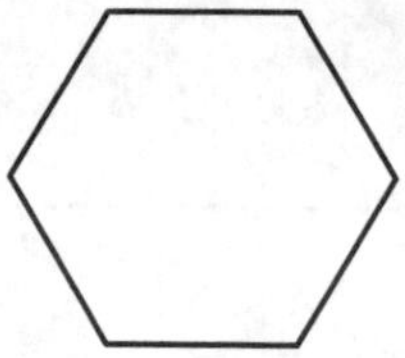 | | | | |
| How many blue rhombuses? 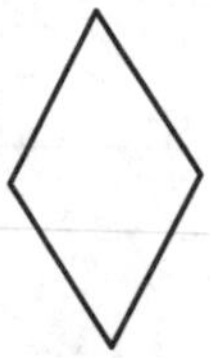 | | | | |
| How many white rhombuses? 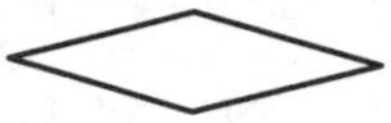 | | | | |
| How many squares? | | | | |
| How many trapezoids? 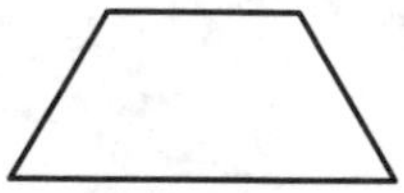 | | | | |
| How many triangles? 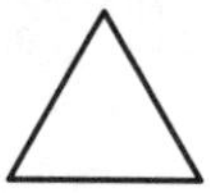 | | | | |
| Draw a picture of the shape you used the most in each puzzle. | | | | |
| Draw a picture of the shape you used the least in each puzzle. | | | | |
| How many pieces did you use in all in each puzzle? | | | | |

NAME _____ | DATE _____

 **How Many Sides? How Many Corners?** page 1 of 2

## How Many Sides?

**1** Trace the numbers.

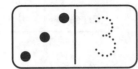  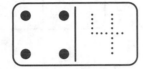  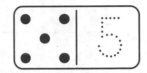  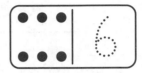

**2** Count and record the number of *sides* on each shape. You can add an arrow on each side if it helps.

| triangle | How many sides? | rhombus | How many sides? |
|---|---|---|---|
| | 3 | | |
| **rectangle** | How many sides? | **square** | How many sides? |
| | | | |
| **triangle** | How many sides? | **rectangle** | How many sides? |
| | | | |
| **square** | How many sides? | **hexagon** | How many sides? |
| | | | |
| **trapezoid** | How many sides? | CHALLENGE circle | How many sides? |
| | | | |

*(continued on next page)*

## How Many Sides? How Many Corners? page 2 of 2

## How Many Corners?

**3** Trace the numbers.

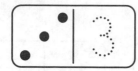 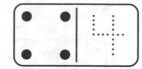 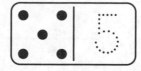 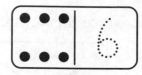

**4** Count and record the number of *corners* on each shape. You can add an arrow on each corner if it helps.

| triangle | How many corners? | rhombus | How many corners? |
|---|---|---|---|
| | 3 | | |
| **rectangle** | How many corners? | **square** | How many corners? |
| | | | |
| **triangle** | How many corners? | **rectangle** | How many corners? |
| | | | |
| **square** | How many corners? | **hexagon** | How many corners? |
| | | | |
| **trapezoid** | How many corners? | CHALLENGE circle | How many corners? |
| | | | |

#  Which Shapes Could It Be? page 1 of 2

## Note to Families

In school your child has been learning how to find a shape by using clues. For each problem, help use the clues, one at a time, to eliminate shapes until just one or two are left that fit *all* of the clues.

Circle all the shapes that fit the clues in each box.

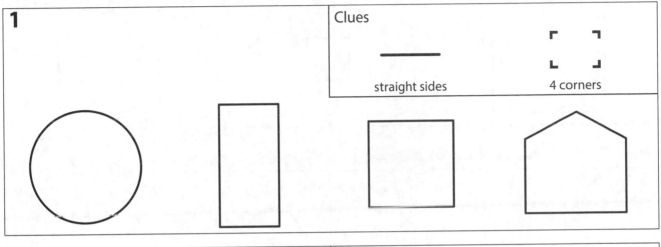

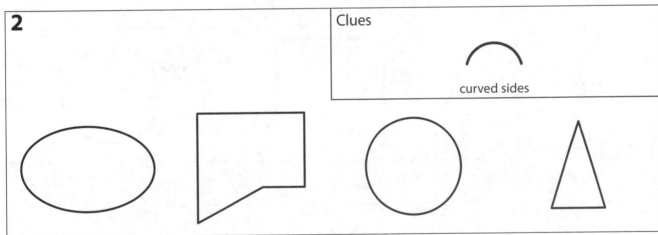

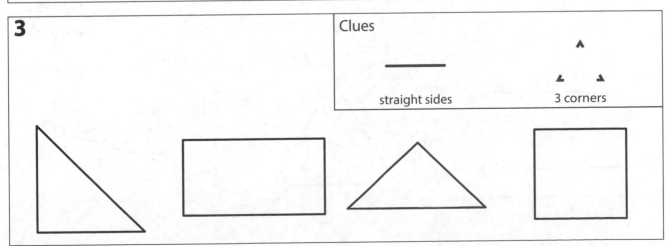

*(continued on next page)*

NAME | DATE

## Which Shapes Could It Be? page 2 of 2

Circle all the shapes that fit the clues in each box.

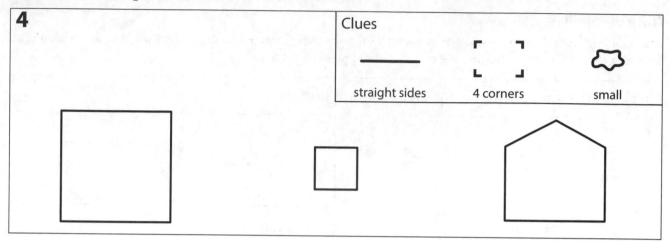

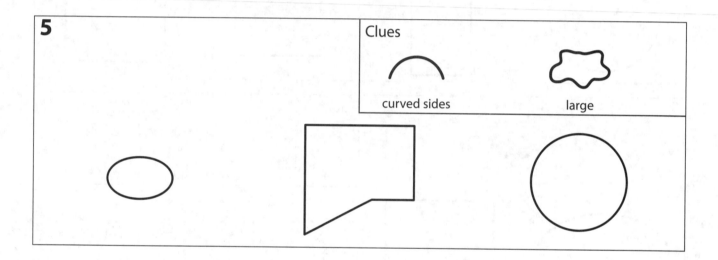

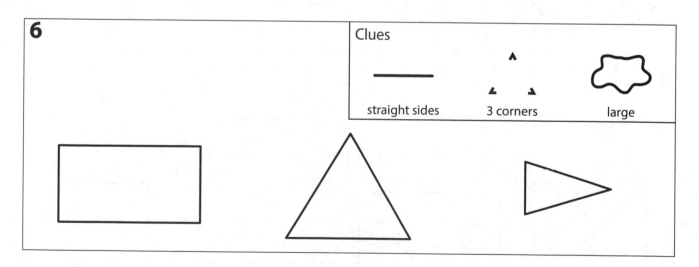

**NAME** | **DATE**

 **Shape Work** page 1 of 2

Draw the three shapes you think should come next in each pattern below.

**1**

**2**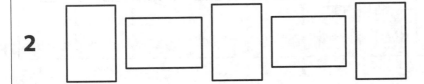

**3**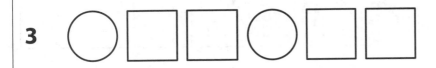

**4**

**5**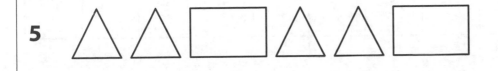

*(continued on next page)*

**Shape Work** page 2 of 2

**6** Count the shapes in each row and tell how many there are. Then fill the rest of the row to make 10 in all. Tell how many more shapes you had to draw.

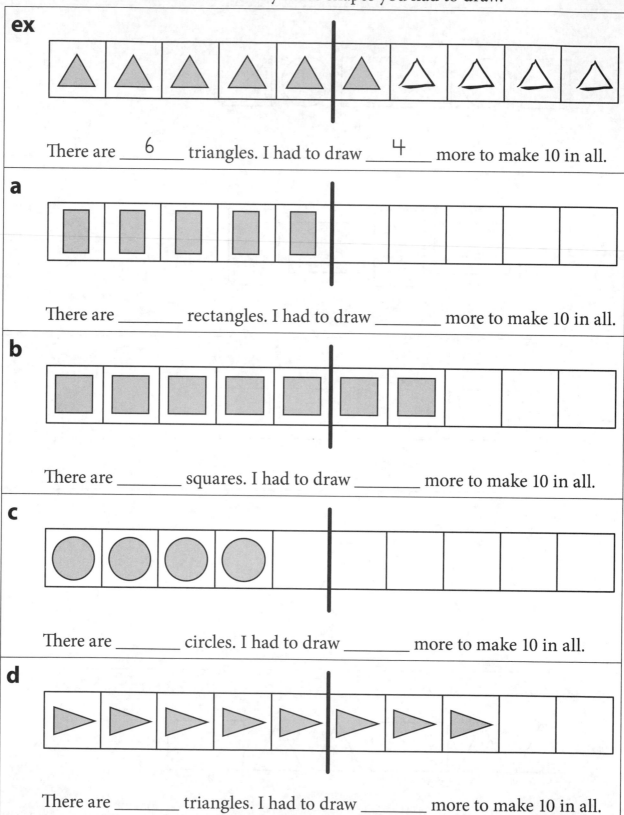

**ex**

There are ___6___ triangles. I had to draw ___4___ more to make 10 in all.

**a**

There are _____ rectangles. I had to draw _____ more to make 10 in all.

**b**

There are _____ squares. I had to draw _____ more to make 10 in all.

**c**

There are _____ circles. I had to draw _____ more to make 10 in all.

**d**

There are _____ triangles. I had to draw _____ more to make 10 in all.

NAME _____ | DATE _____

 **Search for Spheres** page 1 of 2

**Note to Families**

At school, your child has been learning about spheres. Go on a search for objects in your house that are spheres (for example, a basketball or an orange) and count how many spheres you find.

## Instructions

Spheres are all around us! Search around your house for objects that are spheres (for example, a basketball). How many can you find?

**1** In the table below, write the name of each sphere and how many you find.

| Spheres In My House | |
|---|---|
| **Name of Sphere** | **How many?** |
| example Basketball | 2 |
| | |
| | |
| | |
| | |
| | |

**2** How many different kinds of spheres did you find in your house? _____

**3** **CHALLENGE** Miguel found 6 spheres in his room. He found 5 more spheres in the kitchen. How many spheres did he find in all? In the space below, show how you solve this problem.

*(continued on next page)*

## Search for Spheres page 2 of 2

**4** Use crayons or colored pencils to color in just the spheres.

**5** How many pictures of spheres did you color in? _____

**6** **CHALLENGE** Which pictures could you combine to show 20 spheres?

# Cylinders & Spheres Race to Twenty page 1 of 3

## Note to Families

As you play this game, use the words *cylinder* and *sphere* to help your child learn them. Talk about and count how many have been filled in, and remind your child that the heavy black marks indicate five spaces, making it easier to count on from 5 or 10.

## Materials

- Cylinders & Squares Race to Twenty, pages 1–3
- 4 crayons in different colors
- paperclip and pencil (to be used as a spinner)

## Instructions

**1**  Decide who will play for *cylinders* (the ones shaped like a can) and who will play for *spheres* (the ones shaped like a ball), and pick two crayons each.

**2**  On your turn, spin the spinner and color in that many of your shape on your number line. (If you spin 3, color 3 of your shape.)

**3**  Switch colors on each turn so you can easily see how many you are adding together.
   **Note** Sometimes kindergartners will roll a 3 and color in 3 shapes, and then, if they roll a 5 on their next turn, they will color in 2 more for a total of 5. Instead, make sure the player who rolls a 5 colors in 5 more on that turn. Once they get past 5 or 6 filled in, this won't be an issue.

**4**  As you play, talk about who has *more* and who has *less*; how many more or less, and how you know.

*(continued on next page)*

NAME _____ | DATE _____

## Cylinders & Spheres Race to Twenty page 2 of 3

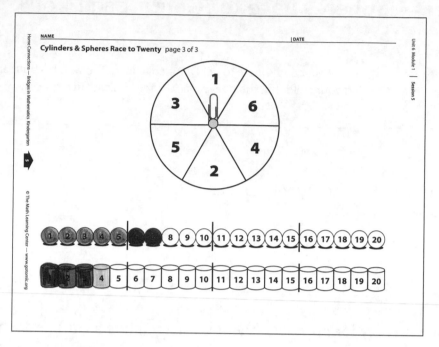

**Parent** *How many cylinders are colored in?*

**Child** *Four.*

**Parent** *How do you know?*

**Child** *Three and 1 more is 4.*

**Parent** *Great. How many spheres are colored in?*

**Child** *Seven… there are 5 and then 6, 7.*

**Parent** *All right. So who has more shapes colored in?*

**Child** *You do. You have 7 and I only have 4.*

**Parent** *How many more do I have?*

**Child** *Let's see… 1, 2, 3* (counting the extras)—*you have 3 more.*

As you get farther along the number line, you can ask, "How many more to get to 20?"

**5** Continue taking turns until all the shapes on one player's number line have been filled in. You need to land on 20 exactly.

**6** **CHALLENGE** Say or write an equation each time you color more shapes. For example, if you had 4 shapes colored and then color 5 more on your next turn, say or write 4 + 5 = 9.

*(continued on next page)*

## Cylinders & Spheres Race to Twenty page 3 of 3

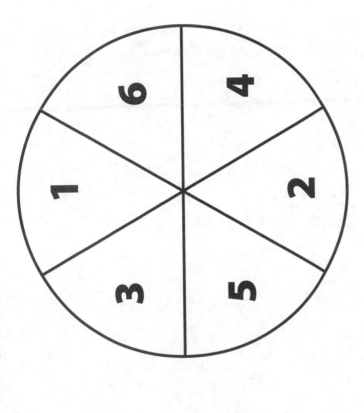

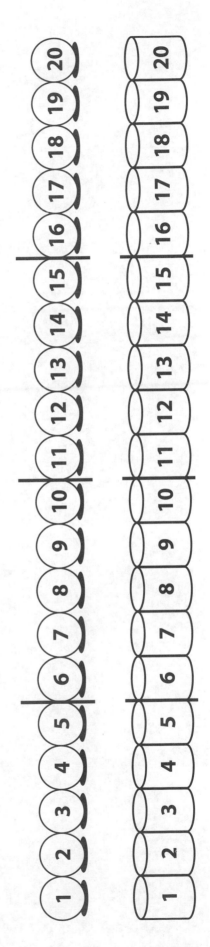

**Shape Bingo** page 1 of 4

## Materials
- Shape Bingo, pages 1–4
- envelope to save the cards
- game markers (pennies, dry beans, small pieces of paper, etc.)
- scissors

## Instructions

**1** Cut apart the two bingo boards on page 3 and the cards on page 4, and get some game markers for you and your partner.

**2** Mix up the cards and put them in the envelope.

**3** Pull out one card at a time. What does the card show? Do you or your partner have a shape on your game boards that matches the card?

**4** If you or your partner have that shape, cover it with a game marker. Cover only one shape on each turn, even if there are several shapes that match the attribute card.

**5** The first person to cover three shapes in a row in any direction is the winner.

**6** Save the cards and play again this week.

**7** Complete the worksheet on page 2 and return it to your teacher.

*(continued on next page)*

## Shape Bingo page 2 of 4

Match the shapes.

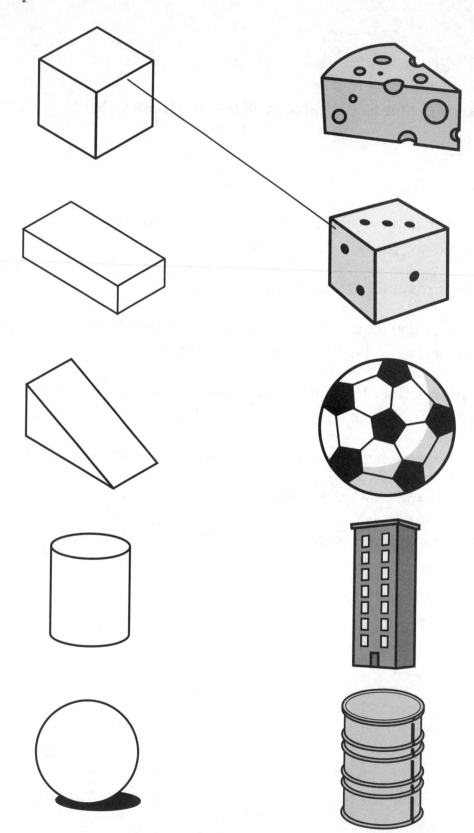

*(continued on next page)*

NAME | DATE

## Shape Bingo page 3 of 4

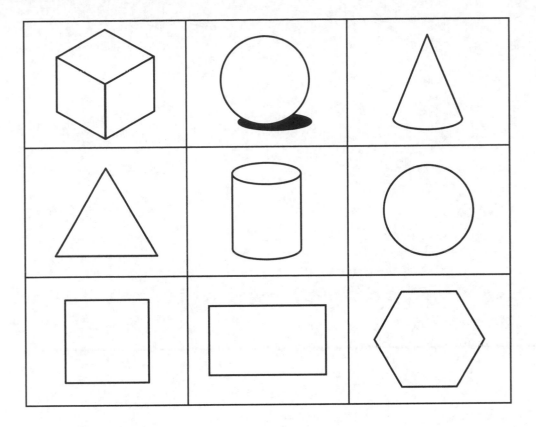

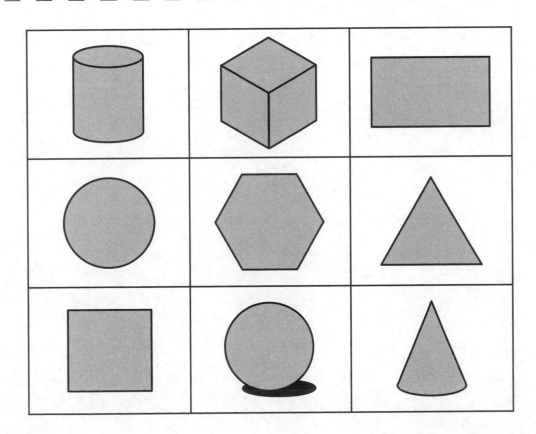

*(continued on next page)*

# Shape Bingo page 4 of 4

## Attribute Cards

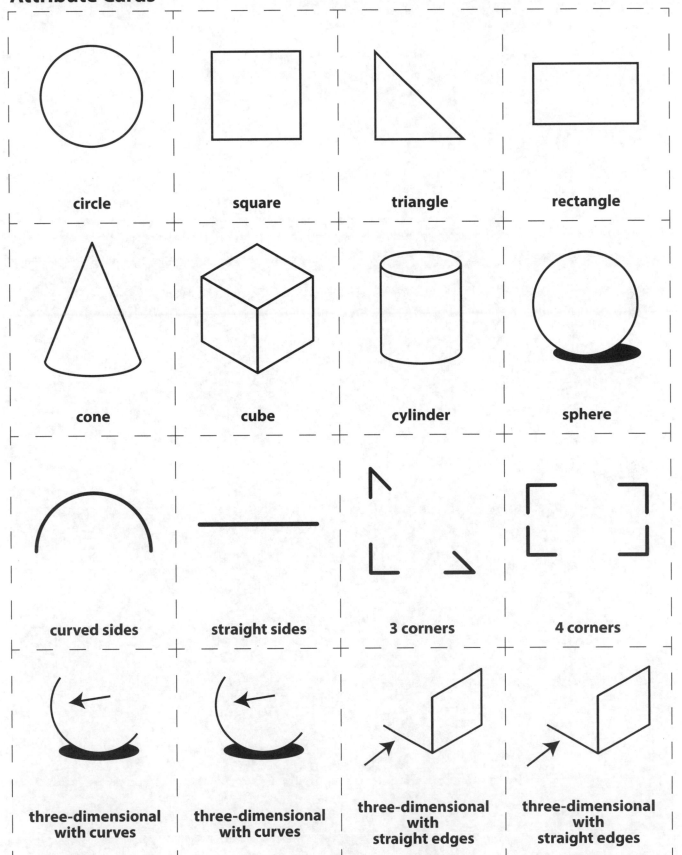

circle     square     triangle     rectangle

cone     cube     cylinder     sphere

curved sides     straight sides     3 corners     4 corners

**three-dimensional with curves**     **three-dimensional with curves**     **three-dimensional with straight edges**     **three-dimensional with straight edges**

**NAME** | **DATE**

 # Shapes & Spinners Graphing page 1 of 4

## Note to Families

In this activity, which we have been playing in school, your child can practice identifying and drawing shapes, as well as making a graph.

rectangle    square    circle    rhombus    hexagon    triangle

## Materials

- Shapes & Spinners Graphing, pages 1–4
- paperclip and pencil for use as a spinner

## Instructions

**1** Use one record sheet (pages 3 and 4) each time you play.

**2** Spin the shapes spinner on page 2. What shape did you land on?

**3** Find that shape on your graph and trace it in the first box at the bottom of the column.

**4** Keep spinning and drawing until one column is filled to the top. Which shape won?

**5** Compare it with the other columns. When you do another graph, do you think that same shape will win again?

**6** Play again on the second record sheet sometime this week.

**7** CHALLENGE

- Keep playing until you have a first, second, and third place winner. Write 1st, 2nd, and 3rd at the tops of those columns.

- When you are done, compare the columns. Write statements to compare two columns. (For example, if you have 3 in the squares column and 4 in the hexagons column, write 3 < 4 and 4 > 3 on your paper.) Try it again with two different columns.

- When you are done, add up two of the columns. Write the equation on your paper. Try it again with different columns.

*(continued on next page)*

NAME | DATE

## Shapes & Spinners Graphing page 2 of 4

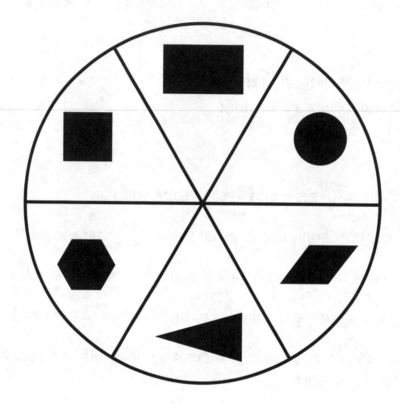

*(continued on next page)*

© The Math Learning Center | mathlearningcenter.org

NAME | DATE

## Shapes & Spinners Graphing page 3 of 4

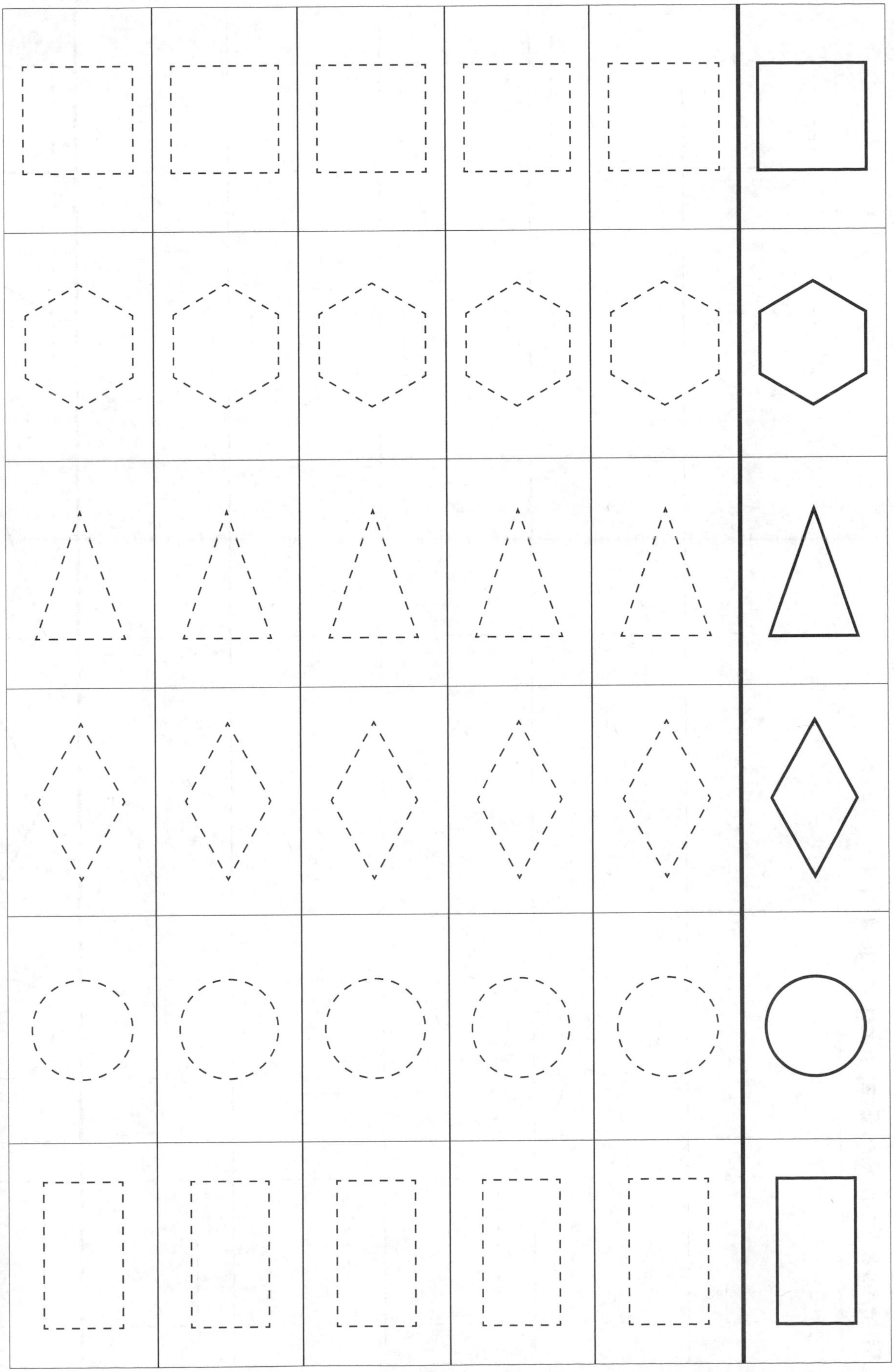

(continued on next page)

**NAME** _____

**DATE** _____

## Shapes & Spinners Graphing page 4 of 4

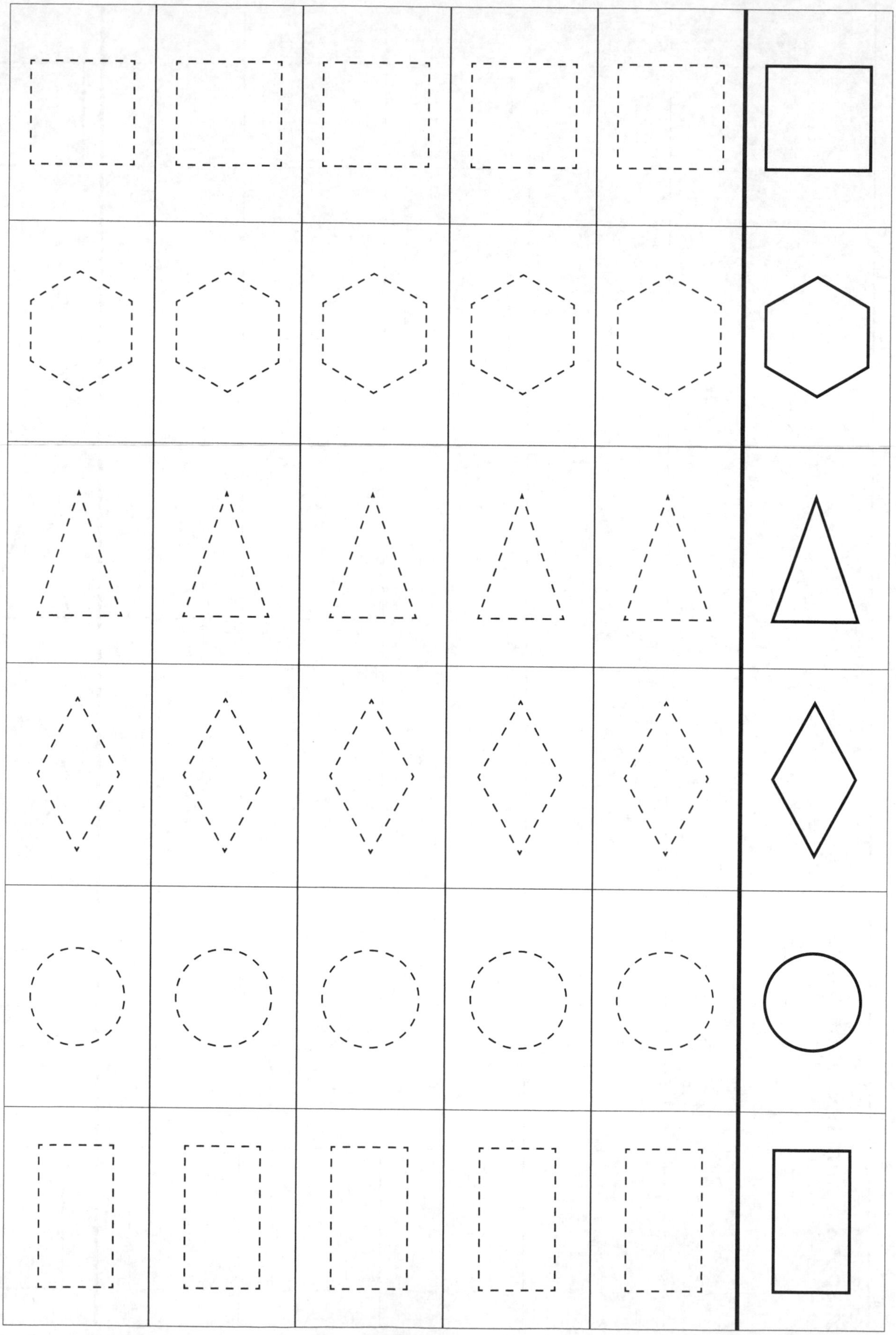

152

**How Many More to Five?** page 1 of 2

Fill in the equations.

**ex**

_____1_____ + _____4_____ = 5

5 = _____ + _____

5 = _____ + _____

_____ + _____ = 5

5 = _____ + _____

5 = _____ + _____

_____ + _____ = 5

_____ + _____ = 5

5 = _____ + _____

_____ + _____ = 5

(continued on next page)

NAME

| DATE

## How Many More to Five? page 2 of 2

**CHALLENGE** Fill in the equations. How many more to 10?

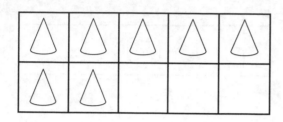

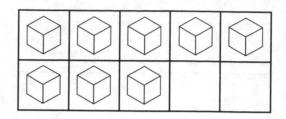

10 = _____ + _____                    _____ + _____ = 10

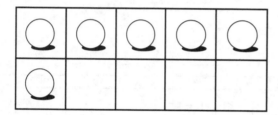

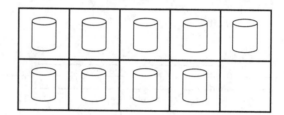

_____ + _____ = 10                    10 = _____ + _____

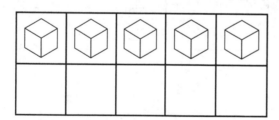

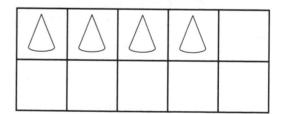

10 = _____ + _____                    _____ + _____ = 10

154

**Ten & More Bingo** page 1 of 4

## Note to Families

When you're playing bingo with your child, encourage counting the cubes on the cards in different ways (by 10s and 1s, by 10s and 5s and 1s, and simply by 1s). It takes some students many times of counting by 1s to really trust that there are 10 in the row.

## Materials

- Ten & More Bingo, pages 1–4
- game markers (pennies, dry beans, pieces of cereal, etc.)
- an envelope for storing the cards

## Instructions

**1** Cut apart the cards on pages 2 and 3 and put them in an envelope.

**2** Cut apart the bingo boards on page 4 and give one to each player.

**3** Cover the "FREE" spot on each board with a game marker.

**4** Take turns reaching into the envelope for a card.
- How many cubes are on the card?
- How did you count them?
- Is there another way to count them?

**5** Both players cover the number on their bingo boards.

**6** The first player to get four in a row in any direction wins the game.

**7** Play the game several times this week.

**8** CHALLENGE
- Play to "blackout"—that's when the entire board is covered.
- Write equations for the different ways you can count the cubes on a card. For example, for a card that shows 16, you could write "16 = 10 + 1 + 1 + 1 + 1 + 1 + 1," or "10 + 5 + 1 = 16," or "10 + 6 = 16," and so on.

*(continued on next page)*

**NAME** _____ | **DATE** _____

## Ten & More Bingo page 2 of 4

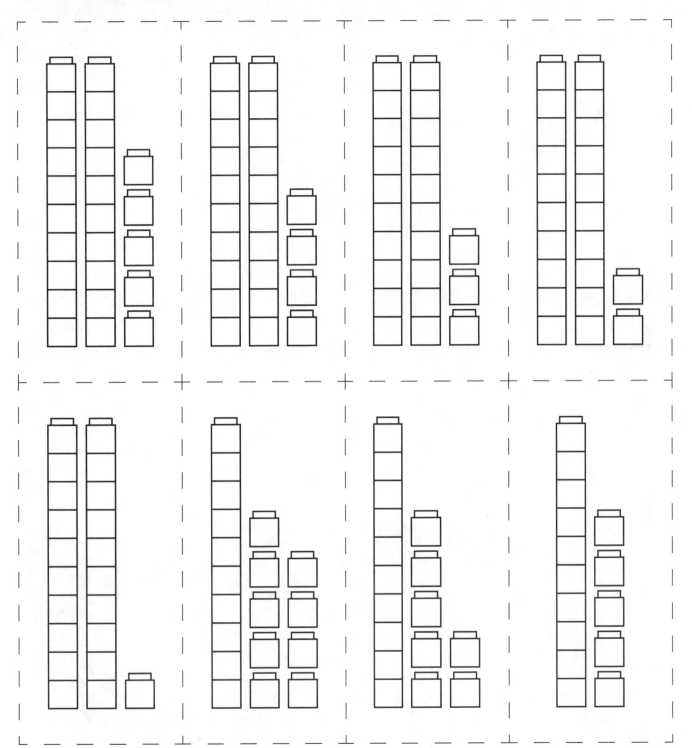

*(continued on next page)*

157

|DATE

## Ten & More Bingo  page 3 of 4

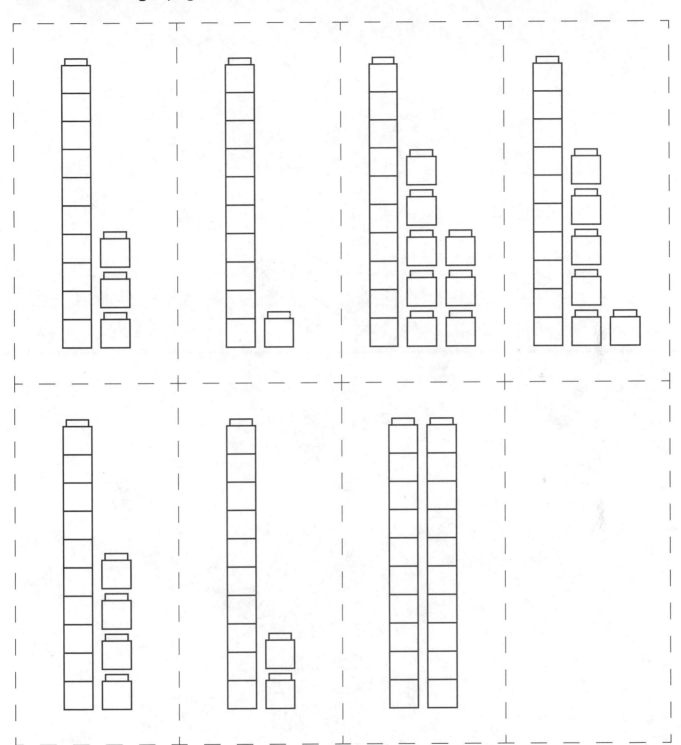

*(continued on next page)*

**159**

NAME | DATE

**Ten & More Bingo** page 4 of 4

| | | | |
|---|---|---|---|
| **12** | **19** | **17** | **20** |
| **21** | **15** | **24** | **13** |
| **25** | **11** | **23** | **18** |
| **22** | **14** | **16** | **FREE** |

| | | | |
|---|---|---|---|
| **11** | **14** | **23** | **21** |
| **22** | **16** | **19** | **18** |
| **17** | **20** | **24** | **12** |
| **25** | **13** | **15** | **FREE** |

##  Race You to 20¢ page 1 of 4

### Note to Families

Be sure to save this game board — you'll be using it again in the next Home Connection.

## Materials

- Race You to 20¢, pages 1–4
- 40 pennies (or any other small item) for 2 players to share
- paperclip and pencil (for use as a spinner)

## Instructions

**1** Decide which side of the game board (page 3) each player will use and who will go first.

**2** Take turns spinning the spinner and collecting that number of pennies. If you land on a nickel, you get to collect 5 pennies.

**3** Set the pennies into the boxes on your side of the game board.

**4** Be sure to wait until one player has finished a turn before spinning again.

**5** Count and compare pennies after each round.

- Who has more pennies?
- How many more?
- How much would the other player need to catch up?
- How many more pennies until each player has 10¢? 15¢? 20¢?

*(continued on next page)*

## Race You to 20¢ page 2 of 4

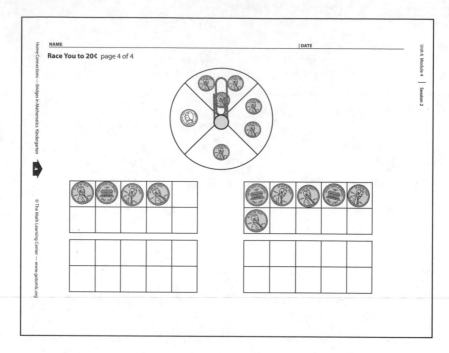

**6** To win, a player must have exactly 20¢. If you spin more than you need, you must wait until your next turn to spin again.

**7** Play the game several times this week.

**8** Complete the What Comes Next? worksheet on page 4 and return it to your teacher. **Note** Save the game board and pennies for the next Home Connection.

**9** CHALLENGE

• Write equations that show the amount you have and the amount you still need. For example, for the game shown above, the player on the left would write 4 + 16 = 20 and the player on the right would write 6 + 14 = 20.

• Write "greater than" and "less than" statements to compare the amounts of the two players. For example, for the game shown above, the statements would be 4 < 6 and 6 > 4.

*(continued on next page)*

NAME

DATE

**Race You to 20¢** page 3 of 4

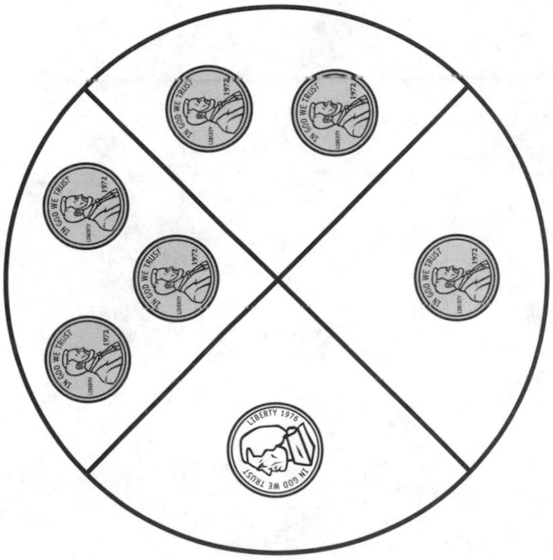

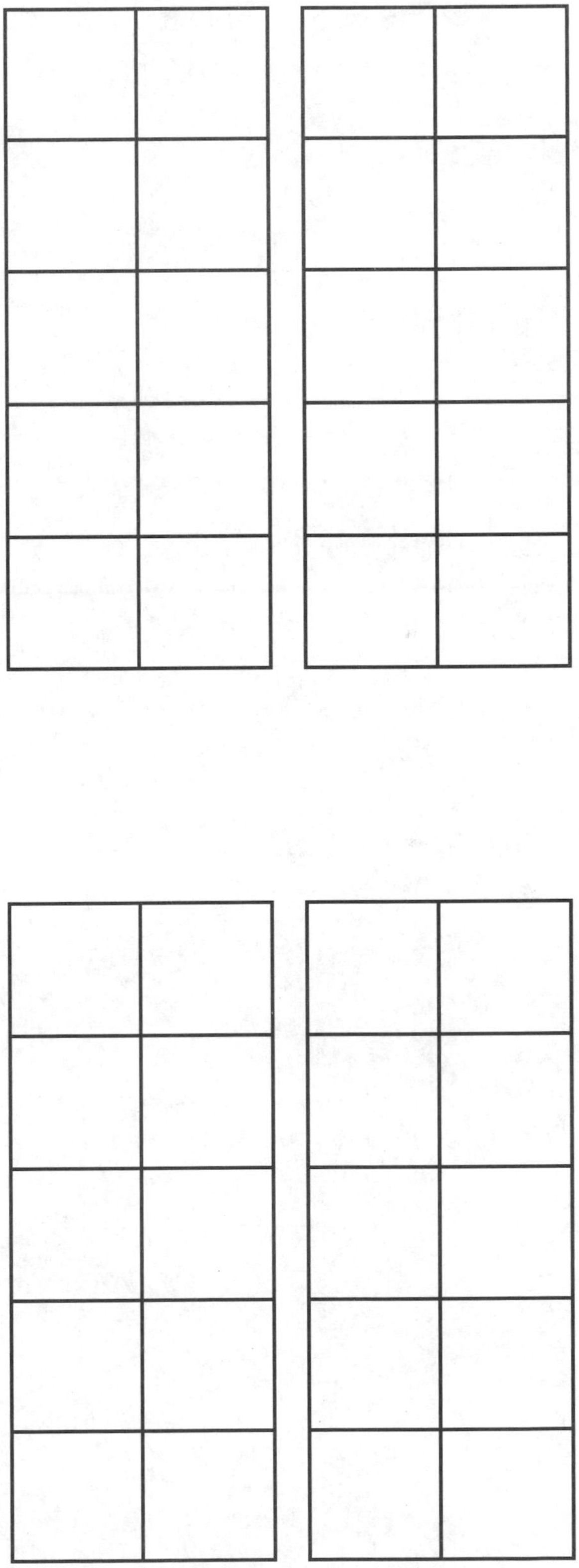

**165**

NAME _____ | DATE _____

## Race You to 20¢ page 4 of 4

## What Comes Next?

Write the number that comes next when you are counting.

| 9    10 | 2 |
|---------|---|
| 6       | 0 |
| 4       | 1 |
| 8       | 3 |
| 5       | 7 |

## Challenge

| 13 | 17 |
|----|----|
| 15 | 20 |

NAME                                                                      | DATE

 **Race You to Zero** page 1 of 3

## Materials

- Race You to Zero, pages 1–3
- Race You to 20¢ game board (saved from the last Home Connection)
- 40 pennies (or any small item) for 2 players to share
- paperclip and pencil (for use as a spinner)

## Instructions

**1** Set 20 pennies on each player's side of the Race You to 20¢ game board to begin the game.

**2** Take turns spinning the spinner and removing that number of pennies from your side of the board. If you land on a nickel, you get to remove 5 pennies.

**3** Be sure to wait until one player has finished a turn before spinning again.

**4** Count and compare pennies after each round.

- Who has fewer pennies?
- How many fewer?
- How many pennies still need to be taken away before each player reaches 0?

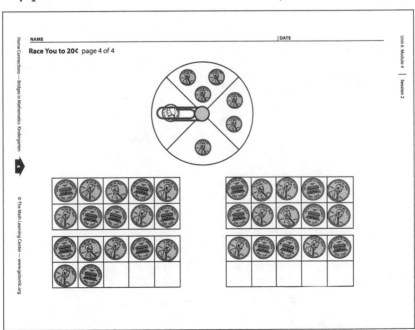

**5** To win, a player must have exactly 0. If you spin more than you need to take away, you must wait until your next turn to spin again.

*(continued on next page)*

**NAME** _____ | **DATE** _____

## Race You to Zero  page 2 of 3

**6** Play the game several times this week.

**7** Complete the What Comes Before? worksheet on page 3 and return it to your teacher.

**8** **CHALLENGE**

- Write equations that show the amount of pennies you still have and the amount you have removed. For example, for the game shown above, the player on the left would write $17 + 3 = 20$ and the player on the right would write $15 + 5 = 20$.

- Write "greater than" and "less than" statements to compare the amounts of the two players. For example, for the game shown above, the statements would be $17 > 15$ and $15 < 17$.

*(continued on next page)*

NAME _____ | DATE _____

## Race You to Zero  page 3 of 3

# What Comes Before?

Write the number that comes before when you are counting.

| 𝟴 9 | 2 |
|---|---|
| 6 | 10 |
| 4 | 1 |
| 8 | 3 |
| 5 | 7 |

# Challenge

| 13 | 17 |
|---|---|
| 15 | 20 |

# How Many in a Pound? page 1 of 3

## Note to Families

Here's an opportunity to give your child something productive to do at the grocery store. Find the scales in the produce section and weigh the items pictured on the record sheet.

## Materials

- How Many in a Pound? pages 1–3
- pencil

## Instructions

**1** Take the record sheet on page 2 and a pencil to the grocery store.

**2** Find the scales in the produce (vegetables and fruits) section.

**3** Find the onions. There might be more than one kind or size; pick just one kind.

**4** Guess how many onions it will take to weigh 1 pound. (Remember, that's how much the sack of potatoes weighed at school.)

**5** Put the onions on the scale one at a time and stop when the scale shows about 1 pound. Record the number of onions on the record sheet. Put the onions back.

**6** Continue gathering and weighing the items pictured and record how many it takes of each to weigh about a pound.

**7** **CHALLENGE** Help the adults you are with to weigh some of the items they need. For example, they might need 2 pounds of oranges or half a pound of broccoli.

**8** At home, complete the worksheet on page 3 and return it to your teacher.

*(continued on next page)*

NAME | DATE

## How Many in a Pound? page 2 of 3

Take this record sheet to the grocery store. Find the scales in the produce section and weigh the items pictured. Record how many of each it takes to weigh about a pound.

**about a pound of onions: how many onions?**

**about a pound of potatoes: how many potatoes?**

**about a pound of carrots: how many carrots?**

**about a pound of bananas: how many bananas?**

**about a pound of apples: how many apples?**

**about a pound of lemons: how many lemons?**

*(continued on next page)*

**NAME** _____ | **DATE** _____

## How Many in a Pound? page 3 of 3

Make a circle around the objects that would be _heavier_ than a potato. Make a box around the ones that would be _lighter_ than a potato.

How many of the objects are _heavier_ than a potato? _____

How many of the objects are _lighter_ than a potato? _____

**Fill It to Five** page 1 of 3

### Note to Families

Your child has played this game in school. Students practice adding numbers to 5 and writing equations.

## Materials

- Fill It to Five, pages 1–3
- pencil and paperclip (for the spinner)

## Instructions

**1** Spin the spinner and add the number to 5.

    **Child** *I spun 4.*

    **Adult** *How much is 5 and 4 more?*

    **Child** *I know it's 5… 6, 7, 8, 9.*

**2** Starting with the bottom box in the appropriate column, write an equation to represent the sum.

    **Adult** *Where should you write the equation?*

    **Child** *Here.* (Points to the bottom box of the column labeled "5 + 4.") *I'm going to write 5 + 4 = 9.*

**3** Keep spinning and writing equations until one column is filled.

**4** Once the game is complete, think about these questions:

- Which equation did I write the most? How many times?
- Which equation did I write the least? How many times?"

**5** **CHALLENGE** Once your child has determined the sum, ask:

- "How many more to make 10?" or "How many more to make 20?"
- "What is __ minus __?" (For example, if the child spins 4, she writes the equation 5 + 4 = 9. Then ask, "What is 9 minus 4?" and "What is 9 minus 5?")

**6** Complete the worksheet on page 3 and return it to your teacher.

*(continued on next page)*

**177**

**NAME** _____ | **DATE** _____

## Fill It to Five page 2 of 3

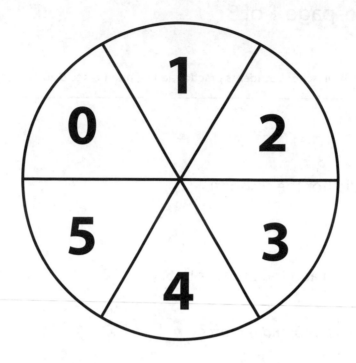

| | | | | | |
|---|---|---|---|---|---|
| | | | | | |
| | | | | | |
| | | | | | |
| | | | | | |
| 5 + 0 | 5 + 1 | 5 + 2 | 5 + 3 | 5 + 4 | 5 + 5 |

*(continued on next page)*

NAME _____ | DATE _____

## Fill It to Five  page 3 of 3

Add (+) or subtract (−). Use counters, ten-frames, or draw pictures if you wish.

**1** Solve each addition problem.

$$
\begin{array}{cccccc}
4 & 5 & 0 & 3 & 1 & 2 \\
\underline{+\,1} & \underline{+\,0} & \underline{+\,5} & \underline{+\,2} & \underline{+\,4} & \underline{+\,3}
\end{array}
$$

**2** Solve each subtraction equation.

$5 - 0 =$ _____     $5 - 4 =$ _____     $5 - 2 =$ _____

$5 - 3 =$ _____     $5 - 5 =$ _____     $5 - 1 =$ _____

**3** **CHALLENGE** Add (+) or subtract (−).

$5 + 5 =$ _____     _____ $= 5 + 3$     $10 - 4 =$ _____     _____ $= 10 - 2$

**Make It Five** page 1 of 4

## Materials
- Make It Five, pages 1–4
- 2 crayons of different colors
- pencil and paperclip (for use as a spinner)

## Instructions

**1** Players write their names on the record sheet on page 3, one above the top section and one above the bottom section.

**2** Player 1 uses the spinner on the next page to spin, and finds the five-frame next to the shape indicated on the record sheet.
- Color in the number of boxes with one color crayon.
- Write the number in the first space of the empty equation next to the five-frame. (For example, if you roll "2 cylinders," color in two boxes of the cylinder five-frame and then write the number 2 in the first space of the empty equation line.)

**3** Player 2 takes a turn, following the directions in Step 2.

**4** Players continue taking turns spinning the spinner and coloring in the number of boxes indicated.
- Once you have used one crayon color in a five-frame, use the second color to fill in the rest of the boxes.
- When a five-frame is complete, finish the equation.

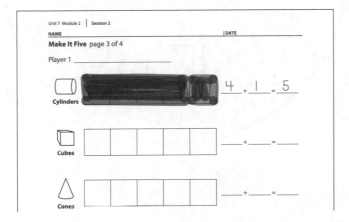

*(continued on next page)*

## Make It Five page 2 of 4

**5** Play until both players have completed all three equations.

**6** **CHALLENGE** After the student has colored in some boxes of the five-frame, cover up the five-frame and ask, "How many more to make 5?"

**7** **CHALLENGE** Without the five-frames visible, ask the following questions;
- What goes with 2 to make 5?
- What goes with 4 to make 5?
- What goes with 3 to make 5?
- What goes with 0 to make 5?
- What goes with 1 to make 5?
- What goes with 5 to make 5?

**8** Complete the worksheet on page 4 and return it to your teacher.

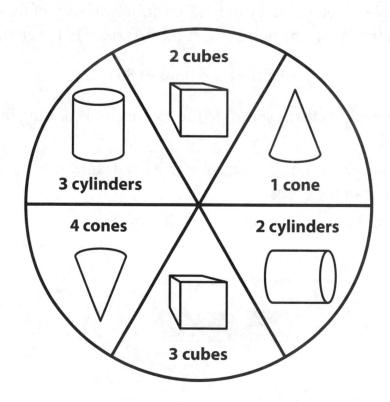

*(continued on next page)*

**182**

NAME _____ | DATE _____

## Make It Five page 3 of 4

Player 1 _____

 **Cylinders** 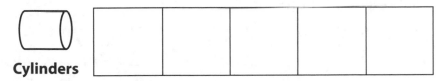 _____ + _____ = _____

 **Cubes** 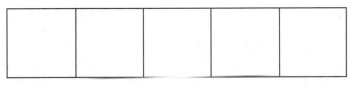 _____ + _____ = _____

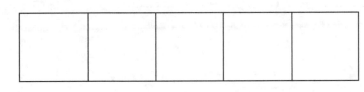 **Cones** _____ + _____ = _____

---

Player 2 _____

 **Cylinders** 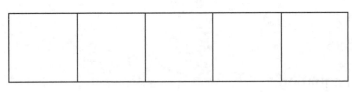 _____ + _____ = _____

 **Cubes** 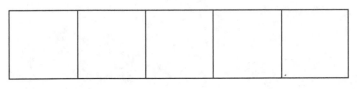 _____ + _____ = _____

 **Cones** 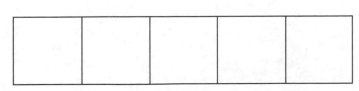 _____ + _____ = _____

*(continued on next page)*

NAME _____ | DATE _____

## Make It Five page 4 of 4

Add (+) or subtract (–). Use counters or five-frames, or draw pictures if you wish.

**1** Solve each addition (+) and subtraction (–) problem.

$$\begin{array}{cccccc}
5 & 5 & 5 & 3 & 4 & 5 \\
\underline{-2} & \underline{+0} & \underline{-5} & \underline{+2} & \underline{+1} & \underline{-0}
\end{array}$$

**2** Complete each equation.

$5 + 0 =$ _____     _____ $= 5 - 1$     $2 + 3 =$ _____     $5 - 2 =$ _____

_____ $= 5 - 3$     $4 + 1 =$ _____     $5 - 4 =$ _____     $1 + 4 =$ _____

**3** **CHALLENGE** Complete each equation.

$5 +$ _____ $= 8$     $5 +$ _____ $= 10$     $10 = 6 +$ _____     $5 +$ _____ $= 7$

NAME _____ | DATE _____

 **Combinations to Ten** page 1 of 2

**Note to Families**

Students have been using ten-frames to help learn the number combinations to 10.

---

Draw a line from each ten-frame to the matching equation.

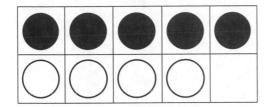

**5 + 5 = 10**

**5 + 2 = 7**

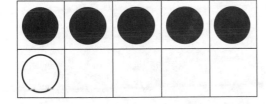

**5 + 4 = 9**

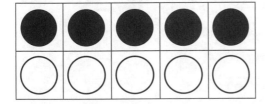

**5 + 1 = 6**

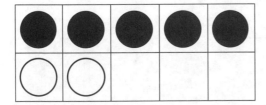

**5 + 0 = 5**

**5 + 3 = 8**

*(continued on next page)*

**185**

NAME _____ | DATE _____

## Combinations to Ten page 2 of 2

Write an equation for each ten-frame. The first one has been done for you.

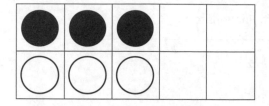

$$\underline{\phantom{3}3} + \underline{\phantom{3}3} = \underline{\phantom{6}6}$$

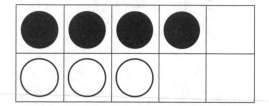

$$\underline{\phantom{xx}} + \underline{\phantom{xx}} = \underline{\phantom{xx}}$$

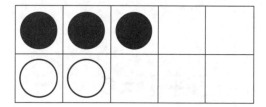

$$\underline{\phantom{xx}} + \underline{\phantom{xx}} = \underline{\phantom{xx}}$$

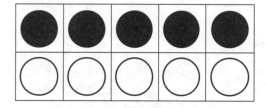

$$\underline{\phantom{xx}} + \underline{\phantom{xx}} = \underline{\phantom{xx}}$$

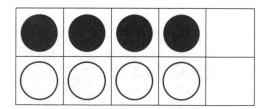

$$\underline{\phantom{xx}} + \underline{\phantom{xx}} = \underline{\phantom{xx}}$$

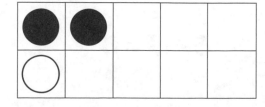

$$\underline{\phantom{xx}} + \underline{\phantom{xx}} = \underline{\phantom{xx}}$$

NAME _____ | DATE _____

 **Capacity Investigations** page 1 of 3

### Note to Families
You will need to have the four containers for this activity cleaned and ready ahead of time. Help your child find them or ask neighbors or relatives if they have some. You may need to read the story problems on the Add & Subtract worksheet for your child.

## Materials
- Capacity Investigations, pages 1–3
- 4 containers similar to the ones pictured at the bottom of page 3
- a $\frac{1}{2}$ cup measure
- scissors and glue

## Instructions

**1** Look at the pictures on the right side of the record sheet on page 3.

**2** Do you have some containers that look like this in your refrigerator or in the cupboard? After the food or drink is used, rinse four containers and save them.

**3** When you have your four containers, cut out the matching pictures and glue them in the boxes on the left of the record sheet (page 3).

**4** For your first container, fill the $\frac{1}{2}$ cup measure to the top and pour it in. Do it again until the container is full, counting each $\frac{1}{2}$ cup.

**5** How many $\frac{1}{2}$ cups did you use to fill the container? Write the number next to the picture. (You may need an adult to write the numbers if you are getting too wet.)

**6** Do it again for the other three containers. Before you start, estimate (use your best guess) how many $\frac{1}{2}$ cup measures it will take.

**7** **CHALLENGE** Do the activity again with one or more of the containers, using a 1-cup measure. First determine how many $\frac{1}{2}$ cups it takes to fill the full cup. Look at the worksheet to see how many $\frac{1}{2}$ cups it took to fill the container, and estimate how many 1-cup measures it will take.

**8** Complete the worksheet on page 2 and return it to your teacher.

*(continued on next page)*

  **187**

NAME _____ | DATE _____

## Capacity Investigations page 2 of 3

**1** Add (+) or subtract (–). Use counters or draw pictures if you wish.

$5 + 3 =$ _____          _____ $= 4 + 4$          $7 + 2 =$ _____

$8 - 2 =$ _____          $10 - 5 =$ _____          _____ $= 6 - 3$

**2** Read the story problems and find out how many.

**a** Katy poured 5 cups of water into the aquarium. The water wasn't high enough so she added 4 more cups.

How many cups of water in all? _____

**b** Aaron put 2 cups of water in his water bottle. Then he added 2 more cups.

How many cups of water in all? _____

**c** The pitcher of juice had 10 cups in it this morning. Marla's family drank 6 cups of juice.

How many cups of juice are left? _____

**d** Darren put 6 cups of water in his dog's water bowl. The dog drank 4 cups of the water.

How many cups of water are left? _____

*(continued on next page)*

## Capacity Investigations page 3 of 3

How many half-cups does each container hold?

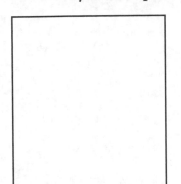

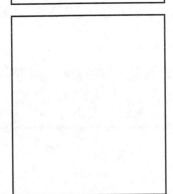

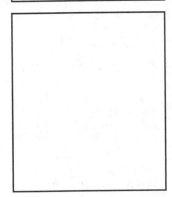

Find 4 containers in your home similar to those below. Cut around the 4 boxes that picture the containers you'll use for your measuring. Glue them in the boxes to the left.

NAME _____ | DATE _____

 **Trains of Ten & Equations** page 1 of 2

### Note to Families

Students have been working with trains of 10 Unifix cubes to learn the combinations of 10 (1 + 9 = 10, 2 + 8 = 10, and so on). We have been using the Unifix cubes to help write equations for each combination of 10.

## Materials

- crayons of two different colors
- pencil

## Instructions

**1** Use two different crayons to color in each train with different combinations of 10. On the line below each train, write an equation for that combination of 10. The first one has been done for you as an example.

$$7 + 3 = 10$$

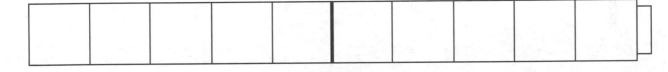

_____

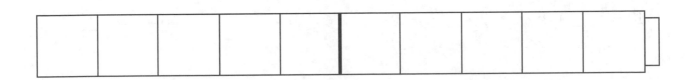

_____

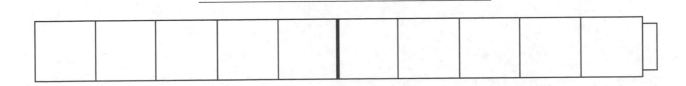

_____

*(continued on next page)*

## Trains of Ten & Equations page 2 of 2

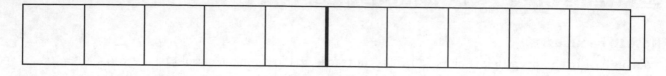

_____

_____

**2**  Add (+) or subtract (–). Use counters or ten-frames, or draw pictures if you wish.

| 5 | 2 | 5 | 5 | 5 | 1 | 5 |
|---|---|---|---|---|---|---|
| – 2 | + 3 | + 0 | – 1 | – 3 | + 4 | – 0 |

5 + 1 = _____          5 + 3 = _____          _____ = 5 + 2          5 + 4 = _____

5 + 5 = _____          8 = 5 + _____          5 + _____ = 6

**CHALLENGE**

10 = _____ + 2          7 + _____ = 10          6 = 10 – _____          10 – 5 = _____

**3**  Write three of your own equations.

NAME

|DATE

 **Double Ten-Frames** page 1 of 2

**Note to Families**

Encourage your student to think "10 and some more" instead of counting all the dots one by one. Ask questions like: How many black dots are there? How many white dots? How many in all? or How many black dots? How many gray dots? How do you know?

**1** How many dots are in each double ten-frame? Write an equation that describes the dots in each one. Circle the double ten-frame that has *more*.

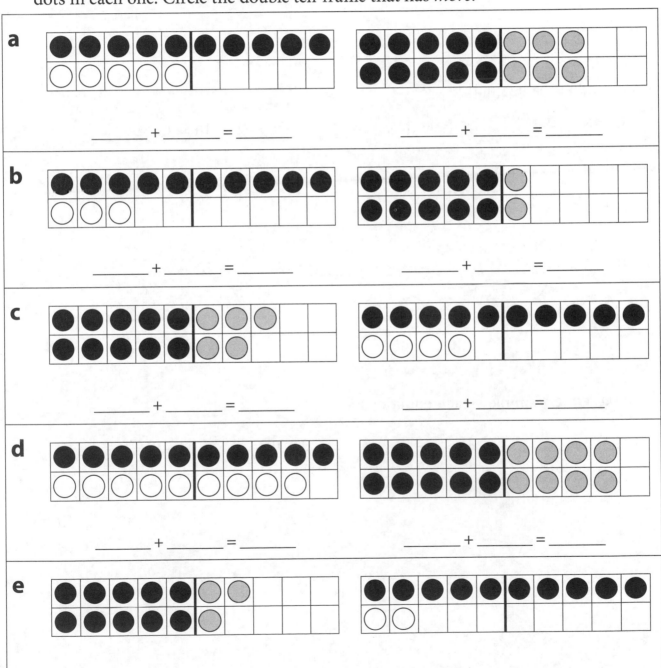

a _____ + _____ = _____        _____ + _____ = _____

b _____ + _____ = _____        _____ + _____ = _____

c _____ + _____ = _____        _____ + _____ = _____

d _____ + _____ = _____        _____ + _____ = _____

e _____ + _____ = _____        _____ + _____ = _____

*(continued on next page)*

NAME _____ | DATE _____

## Double Ten-Frames page 2 of 2

Add (+) or subtract (−). Use cubes, counters, double ten-frames, or draw pictures if you wish.

**2** Solve each problem.

$$
\begin{array}{cccccc}
2 & 3 & 1 & 5 & 5 & 5 \\
+\,3 & +\,2 & +\,4 & -\,3 & -\,1 & -\,0 \\
\end{array}
$$

**3** Complete each equation.

$10 + 1 =$ _____   $10 + 2 =$ _____   $10 + 3 =$ _____

$10 + 5 =$ _____   $10 + 6 =$ _____   $10 + 4 =$ _____

**4** **CHALLENGE** Complete each equation.

$11 − 1 =$ _____   $15 − 5 =$ _____   $20 − 10 =$ _____   $19 − 9 =$ _____

NAME _____  | DATE _____

 **Tens & Ones** page 1 of 2

### Note to Families

Students have been working on counting 10s and 1s in school. Help your child count the bundles of 10 or groups of 10 first, next count the 1s, and then find out how many in all.

**1** For each picture, fill in the blanks to tell how many 10s and how many 1s. Then, write the number in the box that tells how many in all.

**10 sticks**          **1 stick**

| | | **Number** |
|---|---|---|
| **a** | _____ 10s and _____ 1s | |
| **b** | _____ 10s and _____ 1s | |
| **c** | _____ 10s and _____ 1s | |
| **d** | _____ 10s and _____ 1s | |
| **e** | _____ 10s and _____ 1s | |

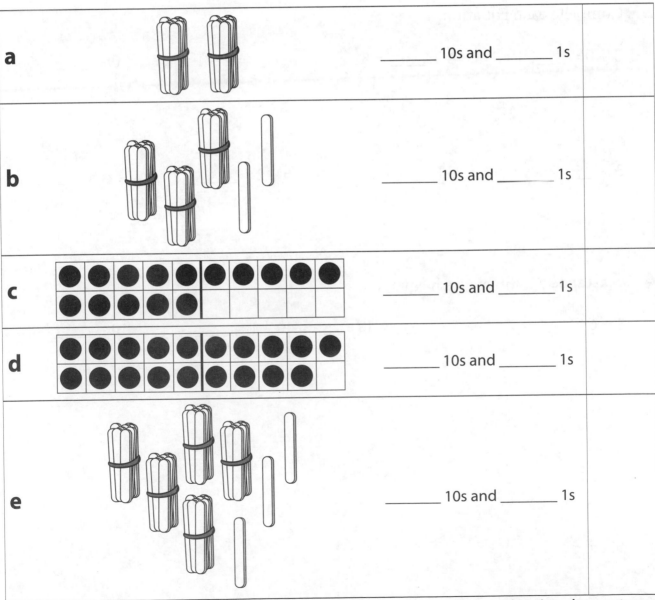

*(continued on next page)*

NAME _____ | DATE _____

## Tens & Ones page 2 of 2

# Combinations to Five

Add (+) or subtract (−). Use counters or ten-frames, or draw pictures if you wish.

**2** Solve each addition or subtraction problem.

$$\begin{array}{cccccc} 4 & 2 & 3 & 5 & 4 & 5 \\ +1 & +2 & +2 & -2 & -3 & -4 \end{array}$$

**3** Complete each equation.

$5 + 0 = $ _____      $4 + $ _____ $ = 5$      _____ $ = 1 + 4$      $0 + $ _____ $ = 3$

$3 + $ _____ $ = 4$      $5 = $ _____ $+ 3$      $5 - 2 = $ _____      $4 = 5 - $ _____

**4** **CHALLENGE** Complete each equation.

$4 + 6 = $ _____      $7 + $ _____ $ = 10$      $10 - 1 = $ _____      $10 - $ _____ $ = 8$

**NAME** | **DATE**

## 🏠 Count the Cubes page 1 of 2

### Note to Families

In these activities your child will record numbers in 10s and 1s. Encourage counting on from 10 ("10, 11, 12, 13, 14"), rather than counting by 1s.

**1** Trace each number.

**2** Count the cubes in each set and record the number.

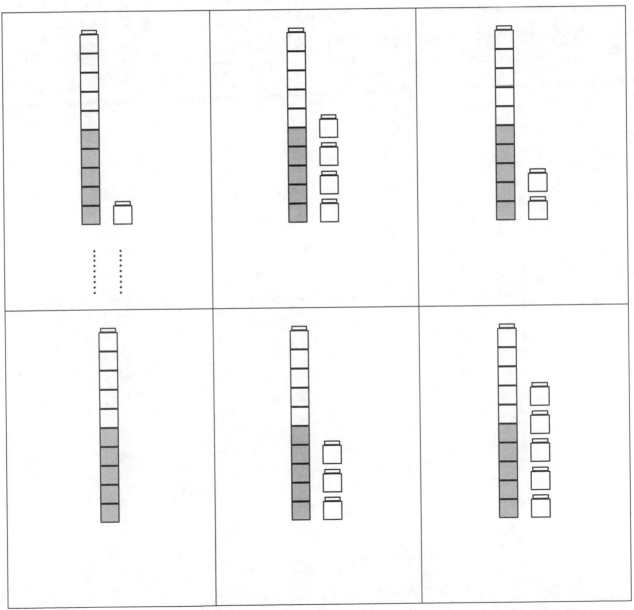

*(continued on next page)*

© The Math Learning Center | mathlearningcenter.org

**NAME** | **DATE**

## Count the Cubes page 2 of 2

**3** How many cubes in each set?

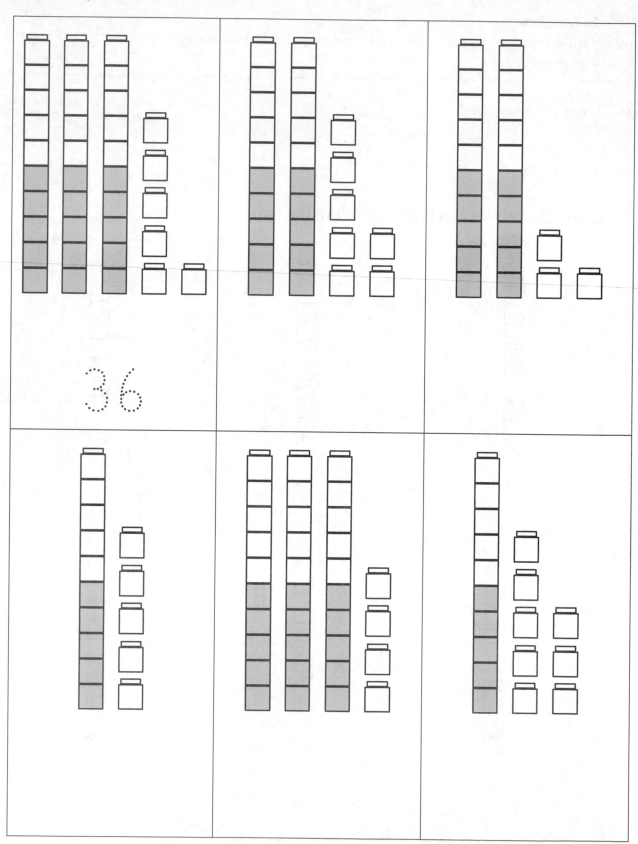

NAME                                                    DATE

## Find What's Missing page 1 of 2

**1** Trace each number.

1    2    3    4    5    6    7    8    9    10

**2** Fill in the missing numbers.

| 1 |  |  |  |  |  |  |  |  |  |
|---|---|---|---|---|---|---|---|---|---|
| 11 |  |  |  |  | 17 |  |  |  |  |
|  |  |  |  |  |  |  |  |  | 30 |

**3** **CHALLENGE** Fill in the missing numbers.

| 31 |  |  |  |  |  |  |  |  |  |
|---|---|---|---|---|---|---|---|---|---|

(continued on next page)

NAME _____ | DATE _____

## Find What's Missing page 2 of 2

**4** Fill in the missing numbers. Use the pictures to help.

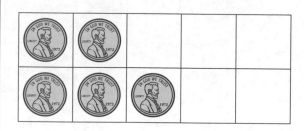

_____ ¢ + 3¢ = 5¢

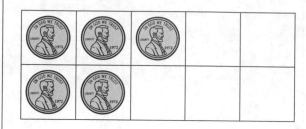

_____ ¢ + 2¢ = 5¢

_____ ¢ + 0¢ = 5¢

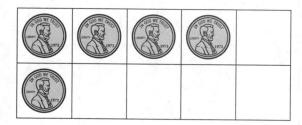

_____ ¢ + 1¢ = 5¢

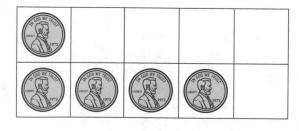

_____ ¢ + 4¢ = 5¢

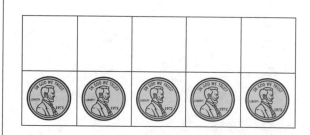

_____ ¢ + 5¢ = 5¢

NAME _____ | DATE _____

 **Frog & Toad Probability** page 1 of 2

**1** On the spinner below, Frog got 6 spins. Toad got 4 spins. Color the graph to show.

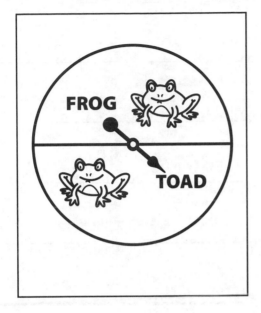

**2** How many more spins did Frog get than Toad?

**3** How many spins did Frog and Toad get in all?

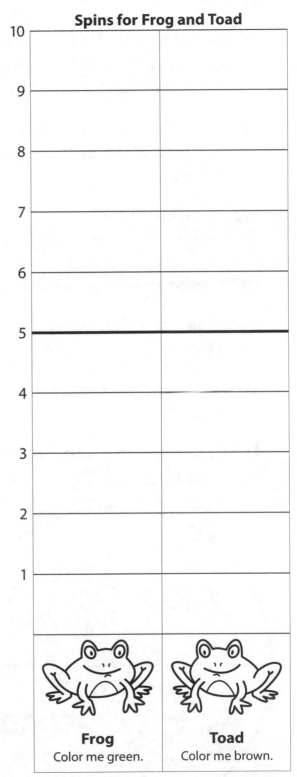

**Spins for Frog and Toad**

| Frog | Toad |
|------|------|
| Color me green. | Color me brown. |

*(continued on next page)*

NAME _____ | DATE _____

## Frog & Toad Probability page 2 of 2

You will need a pencil and a paperclip for the spinner below, and green and brown crayons.

**4** Spin the spinner 10 times.

   **a** Each time it lands on Frog, color one of Frog's boxes on the graph green, starting at the bottom.

   **b** Each time it lands on Toad, color one of Toad's boxes on the graph brown.

**5** Who got more spins?

   ○ Frog      ○ Toad

   How many more? _____

**6** How many spins did Frog and Toad get in all? _____

   **a** How many more would Frog need to get 10? _____

   **b** How many more would Toad need to get 10? _____

**Spins for Frog and Toad**

|  | Frog (green) | Toad (brown) |
|---|---|---|
| 10 |  |  |
| 9 |  |  |
| 8 |  |  |
| 7 |  |  |
| 6 |  |  |
| 5 |  |  |
| 4 |  |  |
| 3 |  |  |
| 2 |  |  |
| 1 |  |  |

**Frog** Color me green.     **Toad** Color me brown.

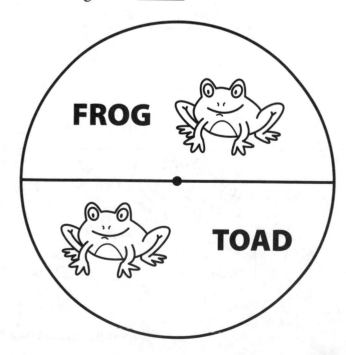

FROG

TOAD

NAME | DATE

 **Frog Story Problems** page 1 of 2

Use pictures and numbers to show how you solve the problem.

# There were 6 frogs but some jumped into the pond. How many jumped into the pond?

*(continued on next page)*

**NAME** _____ | **DATE** _____

## Frog Story Problems page 2 of 2

Use pictures and numbers to show how you solve each problem.

# 4 frogs. How many eyes?

# 10 eyes. How many frogs?

**NAME** | **DATE**

 **Place Value Tens & Ones** page 1 of 2

**Note to Families**

Students have been learning that "-teen" numbers can be thought of as "10 and some 1s." In this Home Connection, they will be matching each double ten-frame with its equation.

**1** Draw a line to match each double ten-frame with the correct equation.

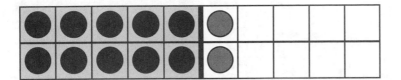   $10 + 8 = 18$

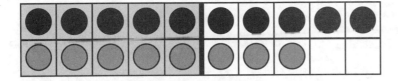   $10 + 4 = 14$

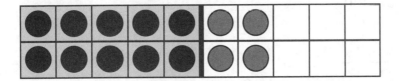   $15 = 10 + 5$

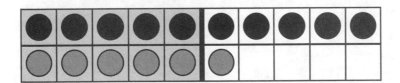   $12 = 10 + 2$

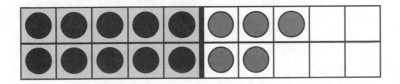   $10 + 6 = 16$

*(continued on next page)*

NAME _____ | DATE _____

## Place Value Tens & Ones page 2 of 2

Add (+) or subtract (−). Use counters or ten-frames, or draw pictures if you wish.

**2** Solve each addition problem.

$$\begin{array}{c} 10 \\ + 4 \\ \hline \end{array} \qquad \begin{array}{c} 10 \\ + 7 \\ \hline \end{array} \qquad \begin{array}{c} 10 \\ + 6 \\ \hline \end{array} \qquad \begin{array}{c} 3 \\ + 2 \\ \hline \end{array} \qquad \begin{array}{c} 5 \\ + 4 \\ \hline \end{array} \qquad \begin{array}{c} 3 \\ + 3 \\ \hline \end{array}$$

**3** Complete each equation.

$5 + 1 = $ _____     $8 + $ _____ $ = 10$     $4 + 6 = $ _____     $1 + $ _____ $ = 5$

$10 + $ _____ $ = 16$     $10 + 7 = $ _____     $8 = 4 + $ _____     $10 = $ _____ $ + 3$

**4** **CHALLENGE** Complete each equation.

$9 + 10 = $ _____     $7 − 4 = $ _____     $19 − 10 = $ _____     $15 − 10 = $ _____

**NAME** _____ | **DATE** _____

 **Patterns & Numbers** page 1 of 2

**1** Trace the numbers.

| 1 | 2 | 3 | 4 | 5 | 6 | 7 | 8 | 9 | 10 |
|---|---|---|---|---|---|---|---|---|----|
| 11 | 12 | 13 | 14 | 15 | 16 | 17 | 18 | 19 | 20 |

**2** Write in the missing numbers.

| 1 | | 3 | | 5 | | 7 | | 9 | |
|---|---|---|---|---|---|---|---|---|---|
| 11 | | 13 | | 15 | | 17 | | 19 | |

**3** How many frogs? Write the total in the box.

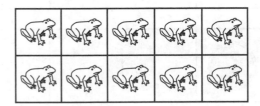 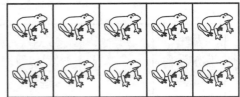 

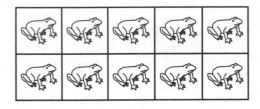 

_(continued on next page)_

## Patterns & Numbers page 2 of 2

**4** Trace the numbers.

| 1 | 2 | 3 | 4 | 5 | 6 | 7 | 8 | 9 | 10 |

**5** Write in the missing numbers.

| 4 | 5 | 6 | | 8 | 9 | | 11 |
|---|---|---|---|---|---|---|----|
| 13 | 14 | 15 | | 17 | 18 | | 20 |

**6** What comes next? Cut out the coins at the bottom of the page and tape or glue them down to show.

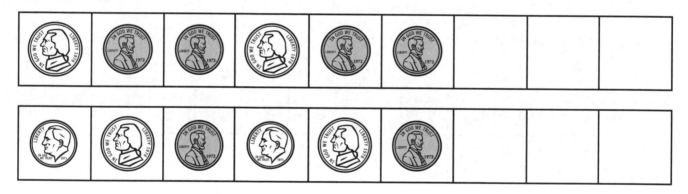

NAME _____  | DATE _____

 **Tens & Ones** page 1 of 2

### Note to Families

Students have been using materials to model and build equations, and matching the models with equations. Read the number words with your child, and point out the repeating "teen" part.

Draw a line connecting each ten-frame with its matching equation and number word. The first one is done for you as an example.

| | | |
|---|---|---|
| | $10 + 5 = 15$ | thirteen |
| | $10 + 7 = 17$ | fifteen |
| | $13 = 10 + 3$ | seventeen |
| | $11 = 10 + 1$ | nineteen |
| | $10 + 9 = 19$ | eleven |

*(continued on next page)*

NAME _____ | DATE _____

**Tens & Ones** page 2 of 2

Add (+) or subtract (−). Use counters or ten-frames, or draw pictures if you wish.

**1** Solve each addition problem.

$$\begin{array}{c} 10 \\ +\ 4 \\ \hline \end{array} \qquad \begin{array}{c} 10 \\ +\ 3 \\ \hline \end{array} \qquad \begin{array}{c} 10 \\ +\ 5 \\ \hline \end{array} \qquad \begin{array}{c} 10 \\ +\ 9 \\ \hline \end{array} \qquad \begin{array}{c} 10 \\ +\ 1 \\ \hline \end{array} \qquad \begin{array}{c} 10 \\ +\ 6 \\ \hline \end{array}$$

**2** Complete each equation.

$5 + 5 = $ _____     $8 + $ _____ $= 10$     $3 + 7 = $ _____     $6 + 4 = $ _____

$4 + 1 = $ _____     $3 + 2 = $ _____     $5 - 3 = $ _____     $4 = 5 - $ _____

**3** **CHALLENGE** Complete each equation.

$11 + 10 = $ _____     $9 - 4 = $ _____     $17 - 10 = $ _____     $23 - 10 = $ _____

**NAME** | **DATE**

## Year-End Interview page 2 of 2

**3** What will you continue to work on during the summer?

**4** Families, what did you notice about your child's math development?

NAME _____ | DATE _____

 **Year-End Interview** page 1 of 2

**Note to Families**

This Home Connection is an opportunity to talk with your child about what he or she learned and liked in math this year. We would also like to hear what you noticed about your child's math development.

Ask your child the following questions and record the answers.

**1** What did you learn in math this year?

**2** What did you like most about math this year?

*(continued on next page)*